RINGO'S RAINBOW JOURNEY

A MEMOIR OF OUR BORDER COLLIE'S
RETURN TO HIS SOUL FAMILY

by Kathy Bolte

Copyright © 2024 by Kathy Bolte

Publishing all rights reserved worldwide.
All rights reserved as sole property of the author.

The author guarantees all content is original and does not infringe upon the legal rights of any other person or work.

No part of this book may be reproduced, stored in a retrieval system, or transmitted in any form or by any means, without expressed written permission of the author.

Edited by Lil Barcaski and Kirsten Winiarski

Published by: GWN Publishing
www.GWNPublishing.com

Cover Design: Aila Designs

ISBN: 978-1-959608-89-9

Dedication

This book could never have been written without the wisdom and guidance of the precious dogs and cats who share their lives with us. Their infinite love fills my heart to overflowing and elicits my profound gratitude for all that they teach me.

Endorsements

What if you could know what your cherished pets are thinking and needing from you? In this book, Kathy shares insights into her pets' inner worlds, channeled by a gifted animal communicator. The information gleaned from these conversations not only improves the animal's lives (and helps Kathy let go when it's time) but becomes transformative for the whole family—human and animal alike.

Prepare to be captivated, holding your breath in anticipation, and blown away as you uncover the remarkable connections that exist between humans and animals. Much spiritual enrichment and meaning can be found in our relationship with our animals if we stop to listen to what they say.

KERI MANGIS, *Author of Embodying Soul: A Return to Wholeness*

This is the extraordinary story of how Kathy and her husband, George, reunite with their beloved Border Collie, Ringo, through the help of a gifted animal communicator. After Ringo's death, he miraculously returns to his soul family in the body of the adorable puppy, Nina.

If you have ever had a heartfelt relationship with a pet, this story will have you laughing, crying, and will leave you with a profound awakening to the infinite possibilities of how our pets love us, and are soul-to-soul connected to us.

Even though I knew the ending before I started, I couldn't put this life-affirming book down until the very last word. As you read it, you'll understand why any skepticism can be completely thrown out the window! This is a remarkable story of a very loving fur-family that you'll remember long after the story ends.

JACQUIE FREEMAN, *Author of award winning Daily Rituals - 30 Days to Peace, Empowerment and Clarity and #1 International Best Seller, Dear Younger Self*

Getting in touch with your own personal brand of spirituality takes time, courage, and patience. And sometimes, it requires setting aside the standard tenants of belief and faith, and opening your mind to something completely unconventional, or out of the ordinary. It's also helpful to be gifted with some sort of guiding light, or spiritual guide, to help you maneuver through your divine journey of life. These beings of light come in many forms and they have different purposes. Kathy Bolte's spiritual guide just happens to be her dog, Ringo.

In Ringo's Rainbow Journey, Kathy shares her story of connection with Ringo–her smart, devoted border collie–who journeyed over the Rainbow Bridge, but refuses to leave her side. Ringo's spirit is reincarnated into her current border collie, Nina, and continues to enlighten and guide both Kathy and her husband, George, through personal relationships, morality, and the age-old question, 'What is my purpose in life?'

One cannot deny the deep connection Kathy has with her dogs, especially Ringo and Nina, and the joy of their many adventures and evolving relationships. Simply put, Ringo's Rainbow Journey is for anyone who loves dogs. Kathy's writing is sharp and playful, but also deep and thoughtful when necessary. She offers humor, comfort, inspiration, and insight into the life lessons our dogs make available to us, exploring such themes as unconditional love, loyalty, our need for connection with nature, fearlessness when facing the unknown, and much more.

LAUREEN PITTMAN, *author of The Lie That Binds; An Adoptee's Journey Through Rejection, Redirection, DNA, and Discovery.*

Kathy is a remarkable communicator of love and truth. She writes with an honest authenticity that leads you to a better understanding of your own truth.

The book you are about to read is more than just an inspirational story. This book is filled with valuable lessons that pull you in and help you drop even more deeply into a connection with your animals. I felt I was pretty in touch with my Fur Babies until the story of Ringo's journey home showed me how to go even deeper.

RAINA IRENE, *author of Because of Josiah – The Sacred Alchemy of a Mother's Unending Bond with Her Son in Spirit.*

Table of Contents

Dedication 3

Endorsements 5

Prologue 13

CHAPTER 1:   I Found Your Puppy. 24

CHAPTER 2:   Sometimes Ignorance Really Is Bliss. 26

CHAPTER 3:   Big Sister Westy. 29

CHAPTER 4:   Let the Herding Begin. 31

CHAPTER 5:   A Scary Surprise. 33

CHAPTER 6:   Ringo's Introduction to Mountain Biking. 35

CHAPTER 7:   Ringo Had Skills. 38

CHAPTER 8:   The Perils of Coyote Poop. 40

CHAPTER 9:   Well, That Was Shocking. 41

CHAPTER 10:   The Growing Up Years. 42

CHAPTER 11:   And We'll Have Fun, Fun, Fun 'Til Your Daddy Takes the Frisbee Away. 45

CHAPTER 12:   The Day That Everything Changed. 50

CHAPTER 13:   Turns Out, It Wasn't George Who Was the Asshole. . 54

CHAPTER 14:   The Best Way to Heal Our Trauma: Love One Another and Find the Fun. 56

CHAPTER 15:	Geez, That Smells Toxic.	59
CHAPTER 16:	Finally... Agility Classes.	62
CHAPTER 17:	Ringo Stopped the Intruder.	67
CHAPTER 18:	Suddenly, Tragically, We Lost Westy.	69
CHAPTER 19:	Matty: Another Sweet Dog Who "Walked" Into Our Lives.	71
CHAPTER 20:	Along Comes Pinto.	73
CHAPTER 21:	And Then There Were Cats.	76
CHAPTER 22:	Car Rides Replaced Hikes in the Canyon.	79
CHAPTER 23:	Solo Needs Help.	81
CHAPTER 24:	How Can We Help Our Solo.	83
CHAPTER 25:	Life Goes On.	87
CHAPTER 26:	It's Time to Talk to Matty.	92
CHAPTER 27:	We Were Blown Away.	102
CHAPTER 28:	Pinto, "The Potty Mouth" Talks to Amanda.	104
CHAPTER 29:	Yep. That's Our Little Blanket Dweller.	112
CHAPTER 30:	"The Park" Becomes Ours.	114
CHAPTER 31:	Solo Makes Her Transition.	116
CHAPTER 32:	Missing Our Sweet Solo.	118
CHAPTER 33:	Tinker Becomes Brave.	133
CHAPTER 34:	Ringo Tells Us: I Only Want to Die Once.	138
CHAPTER 35:	Ringo Leaves His Body.	152

CHAPTER 36: What? Another Border Collie? 158

CHAPTER 37: Matty Misses Ringo. 173

CHAPTER 38: Finding Ringo: The Search Begins. 183

CHAPTER 39: A New Puppy? Whatcha think? 186

CHAPTER 40: Releasing Ringo. 196

CHAPTER 41: Homecoming Day. 198

CHAPTER 42: It's Puppy Time!!! 200

CHAPTER 43: What About Two Border Collies? 202

CHAPTER 44: No Puppies for Sparkles. 207

CHAPTER 45: Don't Miss Me. I'm Right Here. I'm Ringo. 208

CHAPTER 46: Abbie's Turn to Talk with Amanda. 219

CHAPTER 47: Matty Leaves His Body. 222

CHAPTER 48: Matty in the Afterlife. 224

CHAPTER 49: Checking in with Tinker. 227

CHAPTER 50: For the Love of Ringo. 229

About the Author 233

Acknowledgments 235

*A puppy is a puppy is a puppy.
He's probably in a basket with a bunch
of other puppies.
Then he's a little older and he's nothing
but a bundle of longing.
He doesn't even understand it.*

*Then someone picks him up and says,
"I want this one."*

. . . from "How It Begins" by the poet Mary Oliver

Prologue

If you've ever loved a dog, you understand the depth and intimacy of that relationship. You know that each dog is different and brings an energy that is uniquely his or her own.

We love our pups. They engage with our hearts in a way that makes us vulnerable where we might normally be stoic. They garner our emotional strength when it is needed. They are our confidants during our loneliest hours. They cause us to laugh and cry in equal measure.

These precious beings are by our side, or in our laps, giving and receiving love, counting on us to provide for their needs, treat them with dignity, and honor them as members of the family.

When we think of adopting a "rescue dog," we use the term "forever home." We are, indeed, giving them their forever home. They will be with us for their entire lives. We are welcoming them into our homes where they no longer have to worry about how their needs will be met or who will offer them a kind word and a sense of personal security. With us, they find love.

Our dogs live a relatively short life: about twelve to fifteen years. Shorter if there is a health problem, longer if genetics are in their favor. If we are lucky, they pass peacefully at the end of a long, well-lived life. There may be a health crisis or an accident that takes them unexpectedly; and sadly, there are times when we have to help them make their transition with the assistance of our trusted vet.

It doesn't really matter how or when they leave us, we are always devastated. Our hearts are broken. Our fur-child is gone. Our daily routines have imploded. It becomes hard to go on with our work, or enjoy our play. We weep. We move through our grief as best we can. We are crushed by the loss of our precious family member.

After some time, we may discover that we have finally healed enough that our hearts call out for another furry friend. We go to the shelter, or we find the right breeder, and we bring home another pup to love.

Through the course of the relationships we have had with our dogs, there may be one precious being that we recognize as different. The intimate bond we have with this dog is special, even extraordinary. We come to realize that this is our soul dog.

Many of us have been blessed by finding the dog that is our soul dog, that one dog with whom we have a depth of relationship that wasn't there with our other dogs. It's difficult for me to find the right words, within these few paragraphs, to do justice in helping you understand this special connection. But if you've ever had a soul dog, you know.

Ringo was our soul dog, and I have taken on the sacred task of telling you his story.

He incarnated, first as Ringo, and then came back to us as Nina, to teach important life lessons to us humans. He has turned out to be the most profound teacher I have ever had, validating everything I believe about the eternal nature of the soul.

This precious dog turned my deeply skeptical, atheist husband into a believer of the unseen mysteries of life, and awakened in him the understanding that the soul lives on beyond the death of the physical body.

These pages I've written will introduce you to Amanda, the gifted pet communicator who served as the sacred bridge from Ringo's heart and brain to ours. We've always had a connection with all our pets, of course, but this new depth of understanding, gained through Amanda, created an exponential paradigm shift. We have come to know a world that is richer, more profound, and more glorious than we ever could have imagined.

By the end of our story, I think you'll understand what has been validated for me: that we are all spiritual beings having a physical experience, that the soul lives on through many lifetimes, that we truly do have soul families and soul bonds, and that there is such a thing as an "old soul."

Ringo teaches me that there is a sacredness to life, that love is ever-present and lives on forever. The most important thing we are called upon to do is to recognize it and nurture it.

Before we sink any further into the story of Ringo, let me introduce you to *The Miracle of Amanda*.

It sounds pretty bold to name a person a miracle; but for us, Amanda Reister is an honest-to-God miracle. She has changed our lives in the most profound ways.

Amanda is a gifted pet communicator with whom we've worked since January of 2019. Through Amanda, we've had heartfelt conversations with Solo, Ringo, Matty, Pinto, Tinker, Nina, and Abbie, all whom you'll come to know through this story.

To say it is a miraculous event to have a conversation with your dog or cat is undeniable. The experience has gifted me with a quantum leap in understanding. I see my dogs and cats from an entirely new perspective now. I honor them for the sages they truly are.

We connect with Amanda by phone and she connects with our pets by tuning in to their energy. Each time we have a phone call with Amanda, George and I prepare by setting out three things we know we'll need: 1) My cellphone for the call, placed on speaker. 2) George's phone tuned into the recording app because there is so much information that comes through; and we don't want to miss a word. 3) A box of Kleenex to wipe away the tears of astonishment, gratitude, and laughter we've come to know we'll shed during the call.

We have had practical, and even mundane conversations with our animals. We've been given important information about their health and their histories. We've been told so many jaw-dropping details that only we would know, confirming for us that Amanda is the real deal. And, on many occasions, we've been taught profound spiritual lessons by our pets, through Amanda.

But the most important thing we've been guided through is the journey of our beloved Ringo who chose to return to us, his soul family, in Nina's body.

These conversations have validated so much of what I believe to be true about the eternal nature of the soul, and they have turned my husband into a person who is now open to the greater mysteries of our existence.

Ringo has important lessons to teach us about the immortal nature of the soul, about gender fluidity, about love and devotion. He says that humans so often get it all wrong and that we cause conflict where there need be none.

And so, as we move through the pages of this book, I hope you'll be open to learning from this wise dog. I hope you'll come to know that our beloved pets know and understand so much more than we've given them credit for. Maybe you'll begin to see your own dog or cat as a wise being who can teach you so many things, if you'll just tune in and listen.

Kathy and George: East meets West

George and I met in 1983 in an aerobics class. That's what you did in the eighties. You put on your sneakers, leg warmers, and a headband and followed the moves of a teacher who was jumping, running, and stepping to the sounds of Madonna and Wham.

Though immediately attracted to one another, we were also a bit cautious.. I was a student of all things spiritual. I often say that I came out of the womb seeking God. But my path was circuitous and eclectic. It included things like Tarot, the I Ching, numerology, astrology, chanting mantra, the study of Hinduism and Tantric philosophy, and many trips to India to percolate in ashrams, to sit on the bank of the sacred Ganges River and on the shoreline of the beautiful Arabian Sea.

George referred to my whole eclectic ball of wax as "woo woo." He had been a committed Christian in his twenties. Though no longer a Christian, he retained some of the knee-jerk reaction to the teachings that non-Christian spirituality was not to be trusted.

After leaving Christianity in a bitter fight with God, George became an atheist, always ready to be in the critique and denial of metaphysical beliefs in God or spiritual beings. Though I practiced my own unique brand of theism, I was definitely Team Theism and he was Team Atheism. We fondly called our relationship East meets West.

Over the almost forty-year span of our relationship, none of my spiritual practices had any influence on my skeptical, atheist husband. He remained devoutly suspicious and unconvinced of anything he couldn't confirm with facts.

Amanda changed all of that.

The sacred gateway she created for us to know each of our animals on a much deeper level has changed so much for us. We now look at *all animals* differently. We understand that every sentient being has a beautiful repertoire of innate knowing. I can look into the eyes of a dog or cat, a burro or a hawk, and feel a presence I wasn't aware of before. It has made me even more committed to my vegan lifestyle. It has softened George's heart and ushered him toward an acceptance of things that can't be proven.

I can't explain everything that stands behind what I'm going to say next, but here it is: Coming to know animals through Amanda has made me a better person. Yep, it's true. My love for humanity has shifted. I find myself more curious than judgmental. There is a tenderness that guides me. I have become more loving, more empathetic. I, too, have softened.

Our First Call with Amanda

If you've loved and cared for your forever dog as they move toward their end of life, you know how difficult it is to navigate those last tender weeks or months. There are important decisions to be made. How do we best care for them with the time they have left? How do we support their changing needs? And the most devastatingly important question we must ask and answer, when is it time to let them go?

We were living through this difficult stage of life with Ringo. It was January of 2019. Ringo was twelve, almost thirteen. His vision and hearing weren't as sharp as they had been. He was having great difficulty getting up and down, was unstable on his feet, and had become incontinent. We suspected he was in pain much of the time. Our precious old man needed our help more and more, just to navigate the tasks of daily life.

We made an appointment with Amanda, the pet communicator enthusiastically recommended to us by a friend. We wanted to get some guidance about how best to support Ringo. We live in California. Amanda lives in Chicago. Our appointment with her was via a phone call. She holds appointments with people from all over the globe, all by phone.

The phone rang. The voice on the other end was Amanda. Right from the start we found her to be warm and friendly. She didn't seem at all pretentious or "other-worldly." In fact, she seemed like a sweet, kind person whom you'd like to have as a friend.

Amanda knew nothing about Ringo or about us. She didn't know his age or anything about his history. She only had his name and a photo of his face. That's how she connects with animals, through a photo. From there she tunes into the energy of the animal. She began by sharing her thoughts about our precious Ringo:

"He says he's not feeling well but that he doesn't like to talk about it. He doesn't like to acknowledge his pain. He describes himself as strong, dedicated, athletic, agile, loyal, brave, and fearless."

"That sounds wonderful, dear, but why am I feeling such sadness from you?" Amanda asked Ringo.

"Because I'm showing you who I was, all that I used to be, and it makes me feel sad that I'm no longer that dog." He told Amanda that his body was weak and his mind was sometimes not clear. He admitted that sometimes he doesn't remember who he is.

Amanda told us that Ringo's body hurt a lot of the time. He had extreme muscle fatigue. "Sometimes his muscles don't work when he's trying to get up. He has really bad arthritis and joint issues, and nothing is really helping. He says that there is some medication you're giving him that is making him feel foggy. He wants you to know that it's not making a difference in the pain."

She told us that, sadly, his energy felt similar to other animals she has worked with who are preparing for their transition so they start to "go to the other side" to start preparing. They slip into that world for a little bit. "When this happens it might seem like they're not mentally with us, and then suddenly they're back."

Ringo changed subjects. "I love my dad so much. We're one and the same. We're best friends. I am like an expression of him. He is my everything," Amanda told us, sharing his words.

"I miss being my dad's best friend. We used to do everything together. We used to go mountain biking and hiking a lot, but I can't keep up with him anymore. I feel like I'm a twelve-year-old in a seventeen-year-old body. I feel like a dinosaur and I don't want to be like this."

He told Amanda, "My dad is really going to miss me when I'm gone."

"Ringo says that he is struggling with the fact that his dad doesn't have a spiritual practice like his mom does, so when he transitions, that will be it," Amanda said.

"We won't connect in meditation like my mom does with our cat, Solo," he told her.

"When dad looks into my eyes, I know that I am his spiritual connection. My mom doesn't even understand how much my dad needs me.

"As much as I feel like I'm my dad's best friend, I know that my dad has other dogs. Not just other dogs in our home. My dad goes out every day and touches a lot of other dogs."

"Is your husband a pet sitter or dog walker?" she asked (We were amazed that Amanda picked this up. George is, in fact, a dog trainer and pet sitter.) Ringo told her that George gets to have a connection with a lot of other dogs, but it is not the heart connection like what he and Ringo have.

Ringo continued to describe the way he saw George. "My dad is a real strong guy. My mom has her head in the clouds some of the time, but not my dad. My dad knows what's going on in the world. He knows all the neighbors, he reads a lot, he knows when anyone is going to come to our door. He's real smart. My dad enjoys being in the know."

Amanda told us that Ringo liked being in George's energy. "I just like to hang out with my dad", he said, "eat snacks, hang out. Just be."

He shared an example. "I like when we're watching something like football on the TV. I can feel the highs and lows that Dad feels. It's really intense; sometimes his heart rate even goes up when he's watching a game so when I sit close, it's like I can ride his energy. I want as much TV time with my dad as I can get."

"He says he'll enjoy every single moment of it," Amanda said.

Amanda asked Ringo if he wanted to reincarnate. "I don't need to come back. There are other animals in the house but their energy is lukewarm compared to mine. I think the energy of a brand new 12-week-old border collie would be too much for my dad now."

I asked Amanda to tell Ringo that I would be going to India for a month. To that he said, "Okay, I already knew that, but tell my mom to tell dad how much I love him. I love my mom too, but not as much as my dad."

"Are you sure you want me to tell your mom you don't love her as much as your dad?" Amanda asked.

"It's okay, she gets it. We're dudes together."

The tone of Amanda's voice softened when she shared his next words. "I'm okay when it's my time. I'm at peace with making my transition. When I go, there shouldn't be any guilt for dad about being with other dogs. We have other dogs in our home and I want these dogs to completely fill the void for my dad, most especially the smallest dog will be able to do that."

"Please ask him if there's anything else he needs, to make him more happy or more comfortable," I asked her.

This is what he said:

"More TV time with my dad for the excitement of the highs and lows and to hang out with him. I know it's not the same, but it helps to fill the void of where we used to go biking and hiking together." (How could Amanda even know this?) "And tell my mom I don't want to eat healthy. I want some shit food. Just give me some shit food."

Now, since Ringo had mentioned TV, I told Amanda about his habit of standing in front of the TV and barking for us to turn it on. I wanted her to ask him about this. "It's my way to get my dad and me together. It's my way of calling the family together. But it's especially important for my mom and dad to know that it's what I do to get more TV time with dad."

The appointment time we had scheduled with Amanda was done and we ended our call.

To say we were amazed is an understatement. The details Amanda reported to us about the dog that Ringo was in his prime, his current failing health, and depleted energy, the medication we were giving him that was not working, all were completely accurate. His bond with George and his TV obsession were also right on the money. His yearning for the days of mountain biking and hiking, Ringo's description of George as a dog trainer, all true. *How could she know these things?*

We were so excited by all that we had learned. We were already mentally planning our next phone appointment.

We did, in fact, make many more calls to Amanda to guide us through Ringo's end of life, in his current body. As I reveal more of our astounding conversations with Ringo and our other dogs, you'll learn that he decided he did want to reincarnate, to return to his soul family. It is Ringo who has urged me to write this book, to gift you with the important lessons he has to teach us humans. We'll get to all that as you wander through my words, dear reader. But for now, let me properly introduce you to our magnificent Ringo.

OK Ringo, here we go.

CHAPTER ONE

I Found Your Puppy.

I was at work when I made the call. I'd been looking through ads for a couple of weeks when I finally found a breeder out in Adelanto.

Some might refer to Adelanto as the wasteland. Perhaps it could serve as inspiration for a Bruce Springsteen song about the perfect place to throw away one's life. It's a barren place in the middle of the Mojave Desert which, by the way, is the driest desert in North America. If you drive far enough in any direction, you might find honey or goat's milk for sale. There was even a sign for "live red worms." Mostly, there were old buildings on barren dusty land with precarious looking fence lines barely containing cattle.

I think you get the picture. We were driving out to beyond the beyond to find a border collie puppy for my husband who had a newfound burning desire for a furry soulmate.

It all started with a mountain bike ride. George was out on an arduous trail with a couple of riding buddies when they passed three other riders and a border collie. The dog ran ahead and came up to check them out. He ran alongside them for a while, then ran back to his owner. Everyone stopped at the top of a climb to exchange pleasantries: what a beautiful day it was; how much they loved riding this particular trail; what kind of bike everyone was riding. All the regular bike talk. Then the conversation shifted to the cute little black and white dog who was lying down, calmly, beside his owner. The dog's owner told George what a great cycling dog he was. "Doesn't matter where we ride or how far we ride, he stays with us, and he loves it. In fact, we've already gone sixteen miles today. He's a great dog."

George got off his bike and took a little time to interact with the dog. There was some petting, maybe an unobtrusive lick of the cheek, but the dog remained completely attentive to his owner. George was taken by this little dog who was friendly, curious and tireless. As they said their goodbyes and resumed their ride, George watched the dog run away with the cyclists and, for some unexplained reason, he fell in love.

When he got home from his ride, he announced, "I want to get a border collie to go riding with me." And I replied promptly, "Uhhh…no."

We already had a seven-year-old West Highland terrier, "Westy." She was named "Westy" because George found her on the street and, as we were trying to find her rightful owners, we started calling her "little Westy." As it turned out, we never found them so we kept her, and she kept the name.

We had just gone through the unexpected death of Cali, our beloved Cairn terrier, and a year before that, our 14-year-old husky-pit mix, Kiska. I didn't feel ready for another dog and I didn't think my impetuous husband was either. So, we put the topic to bed. But I just couldn't get out of my head how awestruck George had been with the little collie and so I started a clandestine search.

My nature is this: I usually say no first, then soften to yes. I don't know why. Maybe it's because I'm a Cancer and we're inherently cautious. Is it the way of my people? I don't know. But as I searched, just to feel things out, I began to soften. I called George to tell him that I had found his puppy.

"You what?"

"I found your puppy".

"Oh my gosh, really? Really?"

And so, we went on our way to Adelanto to meet Ringo.

CHAPTER TWO

Sometimes Ignorance Really Is Bliss.

We were completely clueless about how to look for the right breeder. We knew border collies were working dogs. They have the distinction of being acknowledged as "the most intelligent breed." But let's not forget that they have been bred to herd sheep, intimidate cattle, and be the rancher's right hand. And they like their work. They like to be kept busy.

If you've ever seen border collies work sheep, you know how intense they can be, how seriously they take their jobs. As they circle around a flock, crouching low to the ground, moving across the land and never taking their eyes off the sheep; they are genetic poetry in motion.

They command the flock's attention with something called "the hard eye." It's a purposefully intense stare that lets the sheep know, without a doubt, who is boss. And sometimes, if the sheep are not paying close enough attention, the dog might snap at the air or even nip a sheep on the butt.

What we know now, that we didn't know then, is that a breeder can create a lineage of dog that has less working drive and, therefore, makes a better companion dog. They will still want a job to do, but they won't become compulsive about "their work." If not specifically bred as companion dogs, they will be working dogs through and through.

What does one do with a working dog if he doesn't live on a sheep farm? Well, that's where mountain biking, endless hours of frisbee, long hikes and agility competitions come in. We felt prepared to offer our border collie all those options. And we were foolishly confident that those things would meet all his needs. What we were too uninformed to know was that the pups we were about to meet were, in fact, from working dog stock. They would, indeed, have a working dog temperament.

When we finally pulled into the breeder's ranch, we saw several make-shift pens holding adult dogs. There was no green pasture to be seen. Everything was dirt, and sand, and dust.

We were led to a larger pen which contained four little white balls of fluff. These were the puppies that were for sale. None of them met our expectation of what our pup would look like. The dog on the trail that George had fallen in love with was the stereotypical black and white border collie. These pups were predominantly white with a few black freckles on their faces, and one or two black ears. Each also had one unique block of black placed somewhere on their white bodies. The pup we ended up choosing—Ringo—had a broad black ring around the base of his tail, hence his given name.

We also had anticipated getting a small female pup. Ringo was a large male.

But what can you do when it's love at first sight?

This little guy seemed to be completely unintimidated. As the breeder took her rake out to show us his drive and focus, Ringo playfully attacked it. He marched confidently up to me and George, announcing that he would be our choice. He communicated clearly with his eyes that he was, indeed, our dog, and that we would be his forever parents.

And so, we paid the money, signed the papers, and loaded the little guy into our car.

We had a long drive back to Riverside. George drove the car and I held this little fluff ball on my lap. After only a few miles on the highway, Ringo appeared to be car sick. He began to wretch and vomited up something on my lap that looked like a tangle of bulky material. Luckily, I had a large bath towel on my lap which caught all the vomit. George pulled over so we could dump the contents of Ringo's stomach onto the side of the road and, upon closer inspection, saw that it was a rag mop. Ringo had eaten what looked like an entire mop head!

There are times when you don't know what you don't know and that's a blessing because you can move through a challenging situation with optimism and hope. This was one of those times. Ringo would become known to us as our *special needs boy*. George gave him the nickname, *"Handful."* He was challenging in all the worst and best ways. What we would come to know was that he was really our soul dog. He would steal our hearts and teach us lessons that no one else could.

Had we known what we were getting ourselves into with the purchase of this pup, we may have backed out of the deal. But sometimes ignorance is bliss. Had we not embraced our little guy on that day, in the impossible town of Adelanto, we would never have been blessed with the magic that was Ringo.

CHAPTER THREE

Big Sister Westy.

Ringo was pretty brave in attacking that rake, but he had never ventured beyond his own family of dogs. His little paws had never felt anything under them but sand. He didn't know what grass or concrete felt like. He hadn't met other humans or other dogs. There was a great big world out there he needed to be introduced to, and that can be pretty intimidating for a ten-week-old pup.

Thank Dog for Westy, ambassador extraordinaire, and the best "big sister" Ringo could have hoped for.

Westy came into our family at a pivotal moment. George and I were going through a rocky point in our marriage. We were feeling distant from one another and, as I'm sure you know, that sucks. We both needed a little extra TLC. Leave it to a little dog to come along and heal everything.

George was driving his jeep down to the market one weekend morning when he saw a little West Highland terrier marching confidently down the street. He pulled over and hopped out of the Wrangler. "Hey, little westy," he said. "What are you doing out here all alone?"

This cute little dog marched over and climbed up into George's lap. He scooped her into the Jeep and brought her home. She was well-groomed and had a collar and tag, but the information on the tag was outdated. No address. Telephone number disconnected.

We made flyers and put them all over the neighborhood and on the bulletin board at our local grocery store. No one claimed her. George had quickly become attached to this little person. She was so happy and friendly. She had a funny little skip in her gait that couldn't help but make you smile. After a couple of weeks, we decided to keep her and this little westy became our Westy.

We already had two other dogs: our beloved Kiska (half Siberian husky, half Staffordshire terrier, aka Pit Bull) and scruffy little Cali, our Cairn terrier. We also had two elder Siamese cats: Suki & Sidd. Adding Westy to the mix was easy. Kiska and Cali and the cats loved her and she loved them. The dogs became a great pack. We logged a myriad of fun adventures with them.

But as the years passed, we lost Kiska to old age and Cali, when she was just nine, to a sudden and shocking total body organ failure. We can't prove it, but we think it was due to a tainted dog food scare that became "a thing" and killed lots of healthy young dogs.

Our hearts were slowly healing from our losses, and we were grateful to still have sweet little Westy who continued to be happy and healthy, and a great anchor for our family. So, it was time to bring Ringo into the mix.

On the day we brought him home, we planned carefully for Ringo and Westy to meet one another. George went into the back yard and sat down on the grass with Ringo in his lap. I'll never forget his big black eyes staring out of that little white face. After some time, he chose to venture beyond George's lap, walk around, and get a taste of the space that would be his back yard. He sniffed the lawn, looked around, and seemed to get comfortable with his surroundings.

After a bit, we let Westy out into the yard. In typical Westy fashion, she walked slowly up to Ringo, sniffed around, gave him a few welcoming licks and a happy tail wag, and welcomed him into our home.

From that day forward, they were fast friends.

CHAPTER FOUR
Let the Herding Begin.

Our home is in a little valley, surrounded by a small mountain range called Box Springs Mountains. There are a few hiking trails in the foothills that provide the perfect place to walk the dogs off-lead with no worries about traffic.

This beautiful mountain range is home to a large herd of wild burros that often meander down into the neighborhood to eat sweet grass from our lawns and munch on selected hedgerows that are tasty to them. The mountains are also home to coyotes, bobcats, gophers, rabbits, and watchful hawks who circle above to zero in on the unlucky mouse or rabbit who will become their dinner.

We love our mountains and feel grateful that we have this little slice of wild beauty so close to our home.

One day, when Ringo was about four months old, we were out for our morning *walk in the wilds*. Just Westy, Ringo, George and I. No sign of coyotes or burros. All was good.

As the pups trotted along in front of us, we noticed Ringo employing an interesting behavior. He would sidle up to Westy on her right side and push her a little to the left with his left shoulder. Then he'd run around behind her, to her left side and push her a little to the right with his right shoulder. He did this a few times then ran around her in a big circle, stopped about five feet in front of her and crouched—low in the front, butt up in the back—and stared intensely at her. This was classic herding behavior.

We were stunned to witness a pup this young, instinctually moving through the "job" genetics intended for him. He was a herding breed. He was herding his sister. Westy, by the way, graciously complied with this exercise of genetics. Her "job" was to be a loving big sister. And here she was playing "sheep" for Ringo.

CHAPTER FIVE
A Scary Surprise.

On another day, when Ringo was about five months old, I was walking him on this same trail. I had invited our neighbor, Georgia, to take this little hike with us to enjoy the morning air.

It was springtime in Southern California and we all take advantage of being outside during this perfect time of year when the mountains are green after winter rains and the wildflowers are abundant.

This hike included Georgia, Ringo, and me. Westy was home, snuggled into her bed, and George was at work.

Ringo loved walking in this area. We later learned, through a different pet communicator, that he called this "The Big Area" and he loved nothing more than to explore everything there, with his nose, with his eyes, with his ears. He loved it all.

We let him run off-lead in the mountains because, at the time, it seemed safe to us, and he really loved to run along the trail, veer off up into the brush, then run back to the trail. He was already an impressive athlete.

He was enjoying his usual pace when he ran into the brush and up the sidehill. He leapt over a large bush and as he landed on the other side, out of my sight, I heard a bark and then some snarling, like you might hear in the beginnings of a dog fight.

Ringo reappeared suddenly and two young coyotes ran out from behind the bush. He had surprised them by jumping into their space.

The coyotes scattered quickly and Ringo came back to me as I called him.

He seemed excited, scared, and definitely surprised by running into these two. I was shaken and grateful that the encounter hadn't turned into something bad. I hooked him up to his leash and we started home.

Ringo's initial demeanor was "let me stay close to mom"; but with each step, his head lifted, his tail curled up, and something told me he was proud of how he handled himself.

CHAPTER SIX

Ringo's Introduction to Mountain Biking.

I need to begin here with a disclaimer. George and I did a lot of things wrong when we raised Ringo. There was so much we didn't know then about how to raise a physically and emotionally healthy puppy. We know better now, and we do better. But then, we were stumbling along, making decisions that were not always in Ringo's best interest.

One of those decisions was to take him mountain biking with us when he was just six months old.

We now know that research tells us not to over-exercise young pups as it may have a negative impact on their musculoskeletal development. There are specific parameters and going on a 15-mile mountain bike ride at six months is a definite no-no.

Having said that, I can tell you that six-month-old Ringo was one hundred percent into it.

One of his first rides was with George and a couple of our riding buddies. They drove up to Angeles Oaks to ride one of the trails in the San Bernardino National Forest. Ringo did an awesome job of staying with the group, running alongside or behind them, exercising his fast little legs.

At one place in the trail, everyone stopped to have a snack and take a rest. Another group of riders rode by and Ringo followed them. George's friends were concerned. "Aren't you worried he'll get lost?" they asked. "Nope," he answered. "As soon as he realizes I'm not there, he'll be back." George got his Canon Sure Shot camera out and sat down in the middle of the trail. Three. Two. One. Ringo came running back up the trail and George snapped one of our favorite pictures of him racing back to "dad." It's framed and sits in George's office to this day.

When they got home that afternoon, Ringo fell fast asleep and his doggy dreams showed me that he was reliving his adventure—heavy breathing, a little yip from time to time, and paws twitching quickly as he ran alongside the bikes in his dreams.

And so it began, Ringo's mountain biking career. From then on, he rode with us at all our "local" rides, but his favorite was Sycamore Canyon.

Sycamore Canyon is a fifteen-hundred acre wilderness park. It is one of eight protected reserves, designated by Riverside County Habitat Conservation Agency. We can thank the cute Kangaroo Rat for preserving our canyon. That little rat is on the federal endangered species list so it's mandatory that we protect its natural habitat. We don't see many of these little guys during our daytime rides, but at night, they're jumping, just like kangaroos, all over the trails.

One night, Ringo decided he needed to herd the rats. He zeroed in on one in particular. This little guy hopped at first, then dashed back to the safety of its hole and dove in. It couldn't disappear entirely, however, because the hole was too shallow. It turned around, raised its head out and found itself eye-to-eye with a forty-pound border collie. Ringo walked up to it, very slowly, crouched down into border collie herding position and gave it the hard eye to make certain the rat wasn't going anywhere. As soon as he was sure it was contained, he walked away as if to say, "my work here is done," and we continued on our ride.

This park is a beautiful example of typical Southern California wilderness terrain. Native vegetation and boulders are abundant. The hills are green and lush during winter and spring months, dry and brown during summer and fall. A creek meanders through the park and there are several rideable wooden bridges that add an extra charm. There are plenty of trails carved into the mountainside, some for slow pleasure rides and some for thrills. We share the park with an abundance of coyotes, rattlesnakes, and red-tail hawks, an occasional white egret, plenty of rabbits, squirrels, and lizards, and a few road runners. Each time I ride or hike this canyon, I feel grateful that we live so close to such beautiful wilderness.

Ringo rode a lot with us at Sycamore and, whenever we went on group rides, he usually came along. One of our riding buddies had an Australian shepherd named Jax who also liked to come along on our rides. He and Ringo became best friends. Their initial greeting was always the same. Ringo would circle Jax, give him the hard eye and that herding nip to make sure Jax knew that Ringo was the boss, then they'd have great fun running the trails together.

One Sunday morning, we met some other friends for a ride. One of the guys brought his German shepherd. As Ringo and this shepherd met, Ringo expected the same greeting he'd thought was routine behavior for meeting any dog. He ran up to the dog, expecting him to retreat and understand the proper canine hierarchy, with Ringo at the top. This dog had a different idea of hierarchy and ran after Ringo who quickly retreated behind George and looked up as if to say, "Whoa, whoa, whoa, this guy didn't get it right! Tell him how this is supposed to go, Dad!"

CHAPTER SEVEN
Ringo Had Skills.

George taught Ringo some skills to keep him safe while on a ride. For one, he taught him to stay with us and not run off on his own. There were, after all, so many rich distractions to call even a focused dog's attention away.

George started by shouting out "this way" whenever they came to a fork in the trail, and Ringo would follow. Once he grooved that behavior well, George began to say nothing at the forks, and Ringo would simply follow. Next step was to teach Ringo to "go right" or "go left" if he was ahead of George on the trail.

Most of the time Ringo was out in front, leading the ride. He knew the many trails well so it was easy for him to choose a line and go. George wanted Ringo to always be aware of where we were, even when he was out ahead. He knew the sound of our bikes close behind him. If that changed, he would immediately look for us and run across the brush to make his way back to the path we were on, dashing to position himself in front of the bikes once again.

Mountain bikers strive to ride fluidly and elegantly. Ringo was all over that. He was usually the most elegant mountain biker on the trail.

Another skill George taught Ringo, in an attempt to keep him safe, was to hit the ground into the "down" position and stay there. All we had to do was say, "Ringo, down!" to bring him to a halt in any situation. Whenever he heard that command, he would immediately hit the ground and stay down until he was released.

The canyon became our favorite "local" for mountain biking, but we also enjoyed *hiking* the canyon with Ringo and Westy. Westy stayed on the trail with us, Ringo ran across the hills, chasing rabbits or coyotes, feeling free and wild. We loved to watch his big, white, athletic body sprinting across the verdant landscape. It was a sight to behold.

George often took Ringo out on his own for a long hike early in the morning, when it felt like they were the only ones in the entire 1500 acres. This was their "alone time," a little break for George, from his chaotic life in corporate America, a man and his dog carving out a few moments of peace in nature.

One morning, as they were hiking through the hills, George heard coyote pups yipping in the distance. He walked toward the sound but Ringo wouldn't follow. This was unusual because he always walked near George on the trail. On this day, he gave George a concerned look as if to say, "Not a good idea, please follow me, Dad. Pups will have a mom."

George respected Ringo's instincts and said to him, "OK, buddy, I guess you know better." Following Ringo's lead, they walked away from the yipping pups, hiking down one hill and up another, when suddenly the coyote mom appeared at the bottom of that hill. She had jumped up on a rock and began to bark ferociously. She was doing her job, creating a pre-emptive warning to protect her pups. But Ringo saw this as a threat. He ran barking all the way down that hill, driving her away. Confident she would not be coming back, he trotted back up the hill and sat at George's side where they looked out at the valley, their valley.

In this moment, George was extremely proud of Ringo because of the way he so skillfully used his instincts. His first instinct was: *I don't think we should mess with coyote babies.* His second: *I will protect you and chase this fierce mother away.* His third: *I will return to you and sit by your side.*

As George reflected on this, he thought to himself, "If I was living in the wild, you're the dog I would want with me."

CHAPTER EIGHT

The Perils of Coyote Poop.

While on the subject of coyotes, let me tell you about one bad habit Ringo had: eating coyote poop. Obviously, that wasn't a healthy habit and, sure enough, it caught up with him... and with me too.

We noticed that he was experiencing some bloody diarrhea so we took him to the vet. A stool sample gave him a diagnosis of giardia, an intestinal infection caused by a parasite. He was given an antiparasitic medication and in a couple of weeks it cleared up. But then, *I got it!*

Yep! I got it from Ringo.

Just about the time he started to get symptoms, and before he got diagnosed, we were out on a bike ride and he was thirsty. Rather than getting off the bike and taking the time to get out his water bowl and water, I just squeezed the pinch valve on my water pack to let him get a drink. I got it a little too close to his mouth and he licked the valve. No big deal, right? It's my dog. I just kind of wiped it off with my hand and took a drink after Ringo.

About a week later I started getting stomach cramps and diarrhea. At first, I thought it might have been something I ate and that it would pass. When it didn't, I went to the doctor who decided I should give a stool sample. I, too, had giardia. I was put on the same antiparasitic medication Ringo took.

In a couple of weeks we were both better, but George and I decided we needed to fix this coyote poop problem.

CHAPTER NINE

Well, That Was Shocking.

We had tried all the training protocols we knew of to get him to stop eating poop. He wasn't listening to "no" or "leave it," so we decided to try a shock collar.

This is the only time we had ever used a shock collar on a dog and didn't know quite what to expect. We are now both anti-shock collar, and anti any non-positive training method for that matter. But at the time we were concerned about his ongoing health. Continuing to let him eat coyote poop was not an option.

We put the collar on him and went for a hike. As soon as he took the poop in his mouth, we hit the shock button remote. He instantly flipped his head up and threw that turd so far out of his mouth that a major league ball player would have been proud. He wasn't hurt, but he sure was shocked and very surprised. When we came to the next deposit of poop on the trail, Ringo walked so far around it that there was no question: poop eating was no longer a satisfying event. From then on, he completely avoided any poop on the trail. Problem solved. And that was the end of us using that shock collar.

CHAPTER TEN

The Growing Up Years.

As Ringo matured, he grew more into his preferences, as I suppose we all do. Do we become more introverted or extroverted? Do we prefer quiet places or the nooks and crannies of life where we can find good company and lots of mental stimulation? Is our solace in our own quiet home or in the amusement parks of the world?

For Ringo, I'd say he was a classic introvert. He could be a social butterfly when necessary, but he most preferred his own company or that of those who were closest to him. If he was forced to socialize for too long a period of time, he always needed a little downtime in his crate to unwind. The experiences that fed his soul were found in nature on the hiking and biking trails and, of course, with his "peeps."

He most definitely preferred women over men. He hated aggressive men and big dogs, and if we ran into them on a walk, he felt the need to drive them away with warning barks that stated clearly, "Don't come near me. I don't like you!"

Ringo loved TV. Whenever he heard the click of the remote, he would come running in and sit down with us to watch whatever we were watching. Two of his favorite shows were "So You Think You Can Dance" and "American Idol." Anything that included dancing or singing, or girls, always delighted him. He would watch with great focus and, I swear, sometimes I could see him swaying a little with the rhythms of the music. Then he'd settle in, lay down in front of the screen, and watch attentively until he fell asleep.

Contrary to this, he hated any male TV character who spoke loudly or acted aggressively. Someone like that caused him to bark and pace and we'd have to change channels. No cop shows or war movies allowed. He was also weary of animals. If he saw any animal on the screen—even an insect—he'd bark as if he was trying to chase it away. Nothing escaped his keen eye. Even cartoon dogs or a silhouette of an animal on the screen would cause concern.

Once we were watching the U.S. Open Tennis Tournament and Ringo barked at the ball boys who kneel on hands and knees at the side of the court so they can be at the ready to retrieve a misfired ball. They looked like dogs to him.

We could no longer watch National Geographic or Animal Planet because Ringo wouldn't tolerate it. He would bark loudly each time an animal, particularly a big dog, was on the screen. I'm pretty sure he thought he was defending his home against these potentially dangerous intruders.

During the 2016 Presidential Debates, Ringo, who was ten years old at the time, showed a marked disdain for Donald Trump and a definite preference for Hillary Clinton. Every time Trump appeared on the screen, Ringo growled and paced. When Hillary was on screen, he would settle. We're a Democratic household, so we thought this was pretty brilliant.

Another thing he seemed to love watching, especially in his elder years, was football games. He seemed really happy to sit at George's feet as they were cheering on the Green Bay Packers.

Ringo's penchant for watching TV grew. At around five o'clock each day, he would sit in front of the TV and bark for us to come turn it on. He couldn't handle the remote himself but if he'd had an opposing thumb he would have chosen his own channels. After a few aborted attempts at dissuading him, we would often turn it on with no volume just to make peace. Nothing seemed to make him happier than when the whole family—George and me, and all our dogs and cats—were gathered round the TV with a big bowl of popcorn, an occasional piece being tossed his way.

Ringo was all about the adventure. First choice: go on one. Second choice: watch one on TV.

CHAPTER ELEVEN

And We'll Have Fun, Fun, Fun 'Til Your Daddy Takes the Frisbee Away.

Ringo had so much energy. A game of *catch the frisbee* would last all day long if he had his way. He never tired of playing catch whether it was a ball or a toy, especially if that toy was a frisbee. He would sail through the air, contorting his body in any way necessary to make the catch.

When he was about six months old, we went to a charity event at a large equestrian center in San Diego, created to raise money for sick children. For a standard entry fee, your dog could "compete" in a number of different events.

This awesome doggy play day was really fun for both Ringo and Westy.

First up was *lure coursing*. This is where dogs chase a mechanized, white plastic lure, zig-zagging around a 600-yard course. The lure simulates the unpredictability of chasing live prey. Chasing it improves their focus and agility. Many dogs love it, especially sight hounds and terriers who are bred to chase prey. As it turns out, border collies love it too.

There was quite a long line to wait for the lure course and as Ringo stood beside George, watching each dog ahead of him, he became so excited he could barely stand it. There was excited whimpering, a bark or two, some antsy dancing paws, and a lot of pacing. And that was just George! Ringo's excitement was ten notches higher. Minimum age to participate was one year, but Ringo was such a big pup, we thought he could pass. Afterall, no one was checking birth certificates.

Both Westy and Ringo proved to be naturals. Westy did a pretty good job chasing it around with her short little terrier legs. Ringo couldn't get enough. Slower dogs couldn't stay close behind the lure and would cut around in diagonals to try and catch the lure. Not Ringo. He stayed right on the moving target, almost catching it several times. In fact, he loved it so much that we couldn't get him to come to us when he had finished his chase and was called off the course. The attendant said this was not uncommon for dogs who love the sport. They are supposed to be "wild to chase."

Next we explored *dock diving*. This is a great sport for dogs who love to run, jump, and swim. In this sport, dogs compete to jump the greatest distance or height from a dock into a pool of water, lured by a thrown toy. Though Ringo loved to run and jump, he hadn't learned to love the water yet. He simply walked to the end of the dock, looked out across the water at the toy being thrown and refused to move. He wasn't interested in competing or watching this sport. We quickly moved on to herding, the exact "job" the border collie is bred to do.

Border collies are natural herders. They've been used for hundreds of years to help keep the farmer's sheep in check. And they do this job with great authority. Bred and trained to get in front of the flock and assert their dominance, they use body language, intense eye contact, and purposeful barking to bring the flock into submission.

We were all excited to see the herding event. We got to watch border collies herd sheep in a big arena. Ringo was an excited spectator. Because of his interest and our curiosity, we headed over to a small pen where he could be evaluated for his aptitude.

We had seen Ringo's herding instincts displayed in guiding Westy down the hiking trails. We wanted to know how he would do in the real world of herding. He was still too young to face a serious flock of sheep, but at this event, the American Herding Breed Association had set up a ring with a small flock of five. This would be his first up close, nose-to-nose meeting with real sheep. They gave owners a brief handler lesson then sent us, with our dog, into the ring. The dog was observed and scores were given. Ringo had solid scores. The feedback was: "Works silently. Runs moderately wide with little distraction. Power is sufficient for the flock. Responsive to guidance. Keeps the stock grouped and regrouped, and adjusts position well." All this was great for a six-month-old pup that had never met sheep. We were told he had excellent potential for herding.

Feeling proud and puffed up about our talented boy, we moved on to seek out more fun.

Next up was the Agility Competition. The agility course was not open to novice dogs. Dog agility is a demanding and complicated sport which takes years of training in order to become proficient. In this sport, the handler directs the dog through a course which includes obstacles such as jumps, tunnels, broad jumps, weave poles, teeter totters, and high, narrow dog walks. The dog runs off leash. No food or toys are allowed on the course as incentives, and the handler can't touch her dog. It's challenging, and crazy fun, for both dog and handler.

George, Ringo, Westy, and I watched with rapt attention as each dog and handler took the start line and ran the course. The goal is speed and accuracy. This sport challenges both the dog and the handler. It is as much a mental game as a physical one for both. It's a great sport for asking a dog to think on his own, teaching him to problem solve rather quickly. It's a high-impact sport, so the dog and the handler must be highly attentive in order to prevent injuries.

After watching, I was hooked. I knew I wanted to learn agility with Ringo, and I hoped that one day we would be able to compete just as these teams had.

We wandered around the grounds a little farther after we watched the agility runs and found another interesting event: *lure coursing with obstacles.*

Just as the name implies, this was a lure course but with jumps and tunnels to negotiate along the way. It was a hybrid of agility and lure coursing. We stopped to watch it for a little while and learned that Jack Russell terriers dominated this sport. One after another, the jacks would dance and wiggle at the starting line until they were released, then race through the obstacles at top speed, chasing after a fake rabbit.

After watching the jacks for a while, we decided we were ready for a break. It was late afternoon and the sun was hot so we sought shelter on a tree-lined grassy hill. Much to our delight, we had positioned ourselves in the perfect spot to watch the Disc Dog (aka Frisbee Dog) Competition. They were just getting started.

We watched a couple of dogs take the field and fly into the air as their person threw the frisbee. Another dog and human took position. The disc was thrown and sailed a good distance as this scruffy little brown and white Australian shepherd ran, hell-bent to catch it.

This was Ringo's favorite sport, and he was in total focus as each frisbee was tossed. As the Aussie's human made the throw, it was too much for Ringo to handle. He twisted his head out of his collar and sprinted on to the competition field to catch that frisbee himself. He got really close and became an absolute distraction for the Aussie. Ringo spoiled what might have been the winning catch.

We felt awful that we had let our pup escape us. We felt horrible that we had messed things up for the Aussie. He got a do-over and we don't know how he placed because we were already walking away and getting ready to make the long drive home.

As we reflected on the day and all the fun our pups had experienced, we talked about "the infamous frisbee faux pas." With some emotional and physical distance, we could look at the humor in the situation. This little border collie pup ran as fast as he could from the side lines to catch the frisbee. It was really kind of perfectly imperfect. George said the only thing that would have made it perfect was if Ringo had actually caught that frisbee.

CHAPTER TWELVE

The Day That Everything Changed.

Ringo was such a happy, affectionate puppy. He seemed to love whole-heartedly. Adventures. People. Other dogs. His demeanor was always confident and curious, afraid of nothing. And then something horrible happened that changed everything.

Young dogs go through something called "fear periods" as they grow. These are times when they are extremely sensitive to bad experiences. The first fear period is at eight to eleven weeks of age, the second is at six to fourteen months.

There is something in dog behavior called "single event learning." As the name implies, it is a single frightening event that happens during a fear period that has a significant and lasting impact for the rest of the dog's life. The bottom line is that it only takes one bad experience to create an intense, permanent reaction to the trigger that caused it.

As an example, if a puppy is frightened by the big, scary trash truck during his fear period, he may be scared of the trash truck for the rest of his life; or perhaps a pup is yelled at and roughly handled by a man while in a fear period, men might be seen as the enemy forever.

I believe most dog owners hope to give their pup the best chance to grow into a healthy, happy adult. Keeping our dogs out of harm's way is an essential part of ushering them into adulthood. George and I thought we were doing that for Ringo, and then something went terribly wrong.

We were out on a routine hike in "The Big Area"—those foothills of the mountains that surround our home. Ringo was just a little over seven months old. In the short three months he had been with us, he had become a confident hiker and was always enthusiastic when the phrase, "Wanna go for a walk?" was spoken.

Westy and Ringo were suited up with their collars and leashes, tails wagging with anticipation of things to come. After we walked deep into the trails, we felt it safe to let them off leash. No traffic. Plenty of room to see an oncoming person or dog. Everything was feeling comfortable and predictable when we suddenly saw a large, dark-brown pit bull out ahead of us. This powerful looking dog was with his owner, a tall grey-haired man who seemed to have things under control.

I felt nervous seeing these two walking toward us. I even said to George, "Do you think we're safe"? He replied that he thought we were. Surely this man would warn us if he thought there might be a problem with his dog.

Suddenly and silently, without warning, the dog was upon us and quickly grabbed Westy, locking his big jaws onto her little body. His teeth sunk into her right side, around her ribcage. He was snarling and shaking her body as we were screaming at the man and pounding on the dog's head and shoulders to try to dislodge him. She was crying out, no doubt in fear for her life.

The dog's owner finally grabbed his dog by the collar. Westy was dangling in the air, held by his massive jaws. George took hold of the dog's face, hitting him on the side of the head and yelling at the guy to make his dog release Westy. It seemed he was unwilling to do anything to help, and it felt like the attack went on forever.

Nothing we were doing would cause this dog to slacken his jaw and free Westy. His owner was doing NOTHING! He just watched the attack as if he had expected it and was pleased by it.

Poor sweet Ringo was witness to the whole thing, shivering and hugging close to my legs as Westy's blood was being flung onto his body. He began to scream in terror, a clear sign of extreme fear as he saw his big sister, Westy, in the jaws of this beast! We had never heard anything like it.

I had my hands firmly on Westy's shoulders and hips as I was trying to pull her away from the powerful jaws. The pitbull momentarily opened his jaw to attempt to move his bite to Westy's throat. In that instant, I pulled her back and, thankfully, out of further harm. The dog's teeth bit into my hand, but, luckily, that bite was superficial.

I scooped Ringo up into my left arm, Westy under my right, and ran away as quickly as I could. George had finally gotten this man to leash up his dog and was now in his face, yelling profanities. I had never seen him this angry.

As I sat by the side of the trail with Ringo shivering and whimpering, and Westy bleeding, I called to George to come so that we could get Westy to the animal hospital as quickly as possible. We had no idea how extensive her injuries were.

In the immediate aftermath of this brutal attack, and in the shock that we were all feeling, George became the pit bull. I couldn't get him to disengage from his rage at this man and his dog, no matter how many times I hollered "Let's go!" All he could do was stand there, yelling profanities into this man's face.

I finally screamed out, "George, you asshole!! Westy is hurt. She may be bleeding to death!! Get over here now!!!" That seemed to break the spell and he ran to me so that we could hasten to the vet.

Westy's injuries were all mendable. There was no damage to internal organs. Her blood loss was not severe enough to cause any long-term damage. She had many ugly puncture wounds that needed treating. A deep cleaning of her wounds, some skillful suturing and placement of a drain to help avoid infection were all done while under anesthesia. A course of IV and oral antibiotics and bed rest created a healing environment for Westy to become whole once again. With time and tender care, thankfully, she did become whole.

Even after this brutal attack, Westy retained her happy-to-know-you spirit. She still had that happy little skip in her step. She was as eager to meet new people and even dogs as she had ever been.

Ringo, on the other hand, learned a lasting lesson that day. Dogs and people that we don't know are to be deeply feared and never, ever trusted. From that day on, Ringo was a different dog.

CHAPTER THIRTEEN

Turns Out, It Wasn't George Who Was the Asshole.

We had a neighbor whose sweet furry companion was a loveable elder German shepherd mix named Reeses. Our neighbor's name was also George. We called him "Dog George" because we always ran into him and Reeses while walking our dogs. It turned out that he called my George "Dog George" too. This became our joke: that there were two Dog Georges in the neighborhood.

After the attack, we told Dog George about what had happened. He told us that Reeses had been attacked by this same dog, on the same trail! He told a similar story to what we had experienced: that the owner of this dog seemed unconcerned by these attacks. When Dog George said to the man, "What are you doing letting your dog off lead to attack innocent dogs?" He replied smugly, "You have a German shepherd. He should know how to fight."

As word of the attack circled the neighborhood, we learned that this dog had attacked a medium-sized poodle and hurt an elderly woman who had been knocked to the ground.

All this was adding fuel to the fire, infuriating us more. This man was a danger to our little 'hood. The Dog Georges joined forces, did a little detective work and learned where this man lived. My George went to pay a visit, presented him with our vet bill and demanded he pay it. We also turned him in to animal control and the Riverside Police Department.

In the end, Westy's vet bill was paid, the dog was quarantined and mandated to be on a leash when out of his house.

From time to time, for years to come, we would see this man and his dog walking around our part of town. The dog was, indeed, always on a leash, but the sight of these two never ceased to produce a shudder at the memory of the violent attack that hurt Westy, and stole our precious Ringo's innocence.

CHAPTER FOURTEEN

The Best Way to Heal Our Trauma: Love One Another and Find the Fun.

As Westy healed physically, we realized we all had some emotional healing to do. The best way we found for our family to heal was to look for the fun in life, and there were plenty of opportunities to find fun.

Our backyard became Ringo's playground. It was just large enough for a good frisbee toss. The perimeter is grounded with tall shrubs and trees hugging a block wall, creating the perfect park-like habitat for a pup to explore. Because we are surrounded by foothills we often had critters like opossums, skunks, raccoons and rabbits paying a visit. Mice and small rats liked to run on the top of the block wall and jump into the shrubs for cover.

Ringo loved to play find-the-critter games. He could always sense when something was in our yard. He'd bark at the backdoor to be let out so he could chase them down. The larger animals were smart and stayed out of the way. They would tree themselves or scamper out of the yard to safety. But the mice and rats were up for the challenge. Ringo regularly gave chase to Mickey and Minnie and their rat cousins, running back and forth, jumping up toward the shrubs again and again until he felt done with the game. He was inexhaustible when it came to playing, and chasing the mice was definitely a favorite game.

People have been told that border collies "need a job" in order to feel fulfilled. In my experience, a "job" is not what they crave. What they want is to be with their humans as much as utterly possible and for those humans to engage with them. Games like fetch-the-ball and frisbee were heaven for Ringo. As long as we would throw, he would be happy to catch.

George decided to make the game of frisbee more interesting for Ringo so he taught him to weave in and out through his legs before the toss. He became incredibly fast as he learned to navigate the figure eight motion. With frisbee in hand, George would simply point his finger toward his legs and Ringo would weave, weave and weave some more until George called "down." Ringo would hit the ground and wait for the frisbee toss, then run as fast as he could to jump up, sail through the air and catch the prize.

As most people do, we had accumulated lots of toys for our pups to play with. There were frisbees, tennis balls, lots of stuffed animals, and chew bones. Squeaky toys were big fun because of the auditory stimulation they provided. Each dog had its favorites. Westy gravitated toward the stuffed animals; Ringo loved the balls and frisbees. We would often end up with lots of toys scattered around the yard at the end of a good play session. And who gathered them up? Ringo, of course. We would simply say, "Get your toys," and he would gather them one-by-one to be put safely back in the toy box on the back porch. We would take a quick inventory and if one was missing we'd just say, "There's one more out there; find it," and he would search the yard until the missing toy was found.

We still hiked the foothills on the same trail where Westy was attacked. We decided we weren't going to let the trauma of that dog and his miscreant owner claim our joy of hiking in "the Big Area." Ringo always insisted we bring a ball along on our hikes. Even out there, he loved to play chase and if no one would play with him, he'd create his own game. He would carry the ball to the edge of the trail, toss it down the hill, then run down to retrieve it. He did this again and again.

Another favorite game on the hiking trail was "Find Kathy." George, Westy, and Ringo would walk ahead; I'd fall behind and find a big boulder to hide behind. After a few more paces, George would look at Ringo and say, "Where's Kathy?" Ringo would take off down the trail to find me. It was so much fun to watch the joy displayed by his full-body wag when he discovered me in my hiding spot.

At the house, Ringo learned to play crate games. No matter which room he was in, if we said, "Go to your crate," he would run as fast as he could to fly into the crate. George saw a YouTube video of a woman who had taught her dog to open his crate door, go in, and shut it behind him. He decided to teach this to Ringo. Within fifteen minutes, Ringo had it down. From then on, he could go into his crate, turn himself around, masterfully take the sock George had tied to the crate door in his mouth, and pull the door closed. I know we all have a tendency to anthropomorphize our dogs, but I swear he was proud of himself for learning this. He loved to show off this trick whenever we asked him.

CHAPTER FIFTEEN
Geez, That Smells Toxic.

We all loved to hike Sycamore Canyon. There were so many trails to choose from and so much for a dog to explore. Because the park was expansive—fifteen hundred acres of wilderness—we usually let Ringo and Westy walk off-lead. Westy's habit was to stay on the trail near us, but Ringo loved to chase the rabbits which often took him running up into the hills. As he grew into his full height and weight, he was a formidable sight: a fifty-pound, stark white, dog running full speed against the green hillside. His athleticism was admirable as he wove himself through the brush, jumped over boulders, making lightning fast turns, and coming close to actually catching the rabbits.

We, who live in Southern California, know that there is a season to be out on these trails and a season to keep our dogs at home because of rattlesnakes. October through March, when the hills are green with winter rains, offer the perfect time to hike. But the weather, during the months of April through September, leaves us with a dry, scorched landscape that welcomes the rattlers. Whether hiking or riding our bikes, we often run into a snake stretched across the trail, soaking up the warmth. We learn that if you leave a rattler alone, simply walking around him, he's pretty docile and won't bother you. But a curious dog can startle a snake and cause it to strike. A little trick we learned was to hike the dogs at night during these hot summer months. This is when the snakes have taken cover and are sleeping under a rock, off-trail. Whenever we did night-hiking we put a reflective vest on Ringo and took powerful flashlights with us so that we could see him easily against the hills.

One of these nights we were hiking with our friends, Chris and Anna. We all had our dogs in tow: Ringo and Westy, and their Weimaraner, Dusty. There was a big silvery full moon out, lighting the way for us to watch Ringo and Dusty running across the landscape as Westy skipped along beside us. We walked on, enjoying the cool evening, chatting each other up when we realized that we could no longer see our dogs on the hillside. We heard barking and suddenly they came running up to us from out of a dry creek bed. They brought with them an extremely toxic scent. It smelled like some kind of harsh chemical that was foreign to anything we were familiar with. It was so bad that it caused our eyes to water.

As they got close, we realized it was Ringo who was enveloped in this awful smell. We could also see that he had deep yellow streaks running along both sides of his face. It looked like he had run through a field of some type of plant that left yellow trails of pollen on his body. None of us could figure out what this horrible smell was. Our dogs had been skunked before, but this smelled nothing like that. We walked down into the creek bed to see if we could find anything there. There were a few homeless encampments scattered throughout the canyon. Had some homeless person created a makeshift meth lab with toxic chemicals? Had the dogs stumbled on to something like that? We were reaching for answers, but we found nothing.

Ringo was scratching at his eyes, foaming at the mouth, coughing and sneezing incessantly so we decided we needed to take him home and put him right into the bath. He seemed to be in so much discomfort that we now treated this as an emergency. Our first priority was to get this toxin off his body. When we arrived home, George carried Ringo straight up the stairs and into the shower. He shampooed Ringo over and over to try and remove the smell. He took his own clothes off and handed them over to me so I could take them downstairs and put them in the washer. After several rounds of shampooing, we dried Ringo off with towels and took him down to his crate to keep him contained while he continued to dry out. His discomfort was now gone and he was exhausted from the excitement of the encounter and the intense bathing, so he settled in and went to sleep.

George and I were content that Ringo would be fine and it was late so we, too, crawled into bed. We had two cats, Tinker and Solo, whose habit it was to sleep with us. When we got under the covers, they would both hop up on the bed. Solo always made her way onto George's chest, licked his nose a couple of times to express her love, then settled in to enjoy the ebb and flow of his sleepy breathing, her little body rising and falling with each of his breaths.

On this night, she jumped up onto the bed to sink into her normal nightly routine, but as her feet hit the mattress her fur flew out in all directions, her tail stiffened straight up toward the ceiling, and she let out a blood-curdling howl, backing off slowly, eyes wide with fear. She had smelled whatever was lingering of the scent on George's body.

When Solo reacted this dramatically, we decided Ringo's encounter must have been with an animal, likely a skunk. We googled "skunk spray" and learned this: "The secretion itself is a yellow oil that will cling to most surfaces it contacts; like all oils, it does not mix with water. Chemically, skunk spray contains as many as seven different volatile compounds (compounds that readily become gas) that are responsible for its repulsive smell." Bingo! A skunk it was.

Solo strode off huffily, to sleep in the other bedroom like an angry wife who could not stand the sight or smell of her husband. Tinker followed because she always basically did whatever Solo did. Westy and Ringo slept soundly, and Ringo woke up the next day emanating that familiar smell of a dog who had been skunked. A few more shampoos, a few more days passed by, and everything was back to normal.

CHAPTER SIXTEEN

Finally... Agility Classes.

After becoming enamored with this sport at the charity event, I waited patiently for Ringo to become mature enough to start agility classes. Soon after he turned one year old, I started looking for a place where Ringo and I could learn how to run an agility course. I found CampWannaQ, right here in Riverside! And what a gem it was.

In agility, a dog and handler advance through levels to obtain a "qualifying" score or "Q" for short. Everyone who gets serious about agility, and starts competing, wants to qualify. This is why our trainers, Nancy and Kay, named their training facility CampWannaQ.

This facility offered everything I was looking for. The large agility area had a graded dirt surface that was completely fenced and secure. It offered all regulation agility equipment; LED lighting for night time use; a large, open set-up area with benches and a shade canopy; and a mini store for water, snacks and supplies for dog and handler. But the best part was learning from Nancy and Kay. They had been competing in agility with their dogs for ten years when Ringo and I stepped into the agility arena. They were experienced, patient, and encouraging teachers.

Ringo was a quick learner. His athleticism and joy of doing things with me made him a natural for agility. He loved it, and so did I. We went to weekly classes so he could learn to negotiate all the obstacles and I could learn to guide him around a course. We also went to the facility a couple of times a week to practice. Classes were fun and we were learning to be a well-synchronized team. Ringo ran the obstacles with speed and purpose, and I improved my handling skills as we progressed through classes.

There was another border collie who attended class with us. For some reason, this dog chose to bark at Ringo, and only Ringo, whenever he ran the course. Ringo liked being focused when he ran and I think the incessant barking got on his last nerve. One evening at class, as all the dogs and handlers were walking the course, Ringo slipped out of my lead, ran after the dog and nipped him on the butt. I guess it was his way of retaliating for all the barking. No harm was done. All was forgiven. We continued practice and the dog never barked at Ringo again.

As we advanced through our classes, Nancy and Kay suggested some "fun runs." These were competition style events where the dogs weren't really competing, but could run a course just to see how they would handle themselves in a competition environment. We decided it would be fun to see how Ringo would do. We went to our first "fun run."

The event was held in a large park in a neighboring city. There were plenty of expansive grassy areas with mature trees offering welcomed shade on a sunny day. I saw birch, crape myrtle, eucalyptus, Chinese elm, pepper trees, and Mexican palms. The spaces under the trees were jam-packed with dog crates and lawn chairs. Ice chests were appointed with drinks and snacks to sustain people and dogs through a long, hot day. The "competition" hosted dogs that were training in agility, obedience, and frisbee. There were two agility courses and one obedience arena set up in the middle of the park, and one large grassy field adjacent to the agility courses dedicated to the frisbee games.

There were vendor booths peppering the area where you could buy all kinds of goodies for your dogs. Collars, leashes, harnesses in a variety of styles and prices, treats, dog food, toys, and frisbees. There was even a sketch artist to create a quick portrait of your pup, like you would get at Disneyland. This was a veritable amusement park for dogs and their peeps.

The variety of dogs we saw that day was impressive. There were Aussies, beagles, lots of terriers—from tiny yorkies to massive pit bulls. There were labs, doxies, shelties, retrievers, great Danes, mutts of all shapes and sizes, and of course, border collies. Some were there to get points for obedience work; some were there to catch the flying disk; and some, like us, were there to practice our agility skills.

We entered Ringo in two courses, both of equal skill requirements. They were different in the placement of the obstacles for the purpose of providing variety to test rookie pups and their humans' abilities to think on their feet.

We did great on the first run. Ringo mastered the course, performing like a more advanced dog. He stayed perfectly attentive in his "sit and wait" position at the starting line until I called "Ringo, tunnel!" He took the tunnel with speed and purpose and followed my lead as I guided him out to take a jump then turn sharply back to the teeter totter and on to a second tunnel. He took three more jumps, zigzagged through the weave poles and raced over the dog walk. I called for him to make one final jump, run back to the A frame and on to finish by running to my side for lots of love and treats. We were so proud of our beautiful big boy.

We walked around the park, looked through the vendor booths, gave Ringo a few big drinks of water and a rest in the shade until it was our turn to run again. We entered the ring and positioned ourselves at the starting line, ready for a second perfect run. This time the first three obstacles were jumps leading to a quick turn to the right for the A frame. Ringo took the jumps then dashed across the ring, running full speed around the obstacles, taking an impressive four-foot jump over the temporary fence that had been set up to cordon off the arena. He had seen the frisbee competition in the adjacent field and decided that it would be a lot more fun than doing this obstacle course. The folks in the carefully organized frisbee arena were dumbfounded. Where had this dog come from?

George was on the sidelines watching our run. He stepped over the fence and went to retrieve our boy. Ringo had great recall so, when George whistled and called his name, our big white border collie came running across the grass as everyone watched. George leashed him up, and we walked sheepishly back to where we belonged in the agility area.

We decided we were done with agility for the day, but wanted to watch a few more of the course runs and check out the obedience trials. As we walked around with Ringo by our side, a few people came up to us to say something like, "Oh my God, that was YOUR dog!" Each comment somehow felt like a pat on the back. Lots of people also said, "Awesome dog!" All things considered, we couldn't help but be a little proud of our mischievous boy and his crazy antics.

Back at CampWannaQ, we continued our classes and practices. All went well for the first year or so, but then Ringo began to exhibit fear. Our classes were at seven p.m. and, as winter set in, the nights grew dark at five thirty. The big LED lights went on for class, creating shadows over the course. Ringo didn't like the shadows. He began to refuse to practice. His fear got so bad that he started to tremble when we drove into the parking lot. We stopped taking him to group classes and started doing private lessons during the day. He loved being "the only dog" and began to thrive again. Soon our private lessons became semi-private as we met with one other dog—a cute little pug that happened to be a great agility dog and became a welcomed friend to our special-needs boy.

Things started to shift for Ringo around that time. Whenever we were out on a walk, or in any situation where he was asked to encounter a new dog, he showed fear-based aggression. He never bit a dog or a person, but he would growl upon feeling threatened. He leapt toward whatever was threatening to him, stomp both paws on the ground as a warning not to come closer. And who could blame him when, as a young pup, he had witnessed a random dog attack Westy. A happy day had suddenly turned brutal. Ringo's paradigm, as he grew into his maturity, was that he always had to be on guard.

We tried another fun run but when he got in the ring there were dogs walking by the outside of the ring or standing with their handlers simply watching our run. Ringo would break off course and run to the fence to give an aggressive "get away" lunge and bark at the other dogs. This was not acceptable. He was viewed as an aggressive dog and we were not welcome. We had to give up our dreams of competing.

CHAPTER SEVENTEEN
Ringo Stopped the Intruder.

Other than meeting new dogs, there were a couple of random things that were scary to Ringo. For some reason he hated the sound of George sneezing. George was never a one-and-done sneezer. His sneezing attacks always produced six or more sneezes in a row. Ringo could sense when George's breathing was changing to produce a sneeze and he'd run out of the room and stay out of sight until all the sneezing was done.

Somewhere along the line, Ringo decided there was a scary monster living in our downstairs guest bedroom. The window to this bedroom looked out onto the back patio. When passing the window, Ringo would make a big arc around it, side glancing at it all the way, being careful not to get too close. Sometimes he would stand in front of it and bark as though he was trying to drive off a stranger. We never figured out what it was that produced this fear. We all just accepted that Ringo needed to avoid the demon in the window.

Ringo endured his quirky bits of fear; he just worked his way around them, but he was always brave when he needed to be.

One Thanksgiving, long after the family had gathered, the feast had been eaten and everyone had gone back to their own homes, George and I were ready to put our food-comatose bodies to bed. The dogs were ready for bed too. There had been a lot of extra people to play with and get love from, and a few bites of turkey for each pup to enjoy.

Ringo was going through a stage where he liked sleeping in the garage in lieu of his cozy indoor bed. We moved through our nighttime routine of "one last potty, one last drink, and then to bed." We were all sound asleep—Westy in her indoor crate, Ringo in the garage, George and I upstairs in bed—when Ringo began barking loudly. It was two in the morning. George jumped out of bed and went to look out the office window that overlooked our driveway. He saw a tallish man with a slender build running down the driveway and onto our street. George dashed downstairs and out the front door to give chase to this apparent intruder. The night was foggy so George quickly lost sight of him and gave up the search. He came back in the house and went out to the garage to check in on Ringo who was still amped, ready to be of service. George gave Ringo lots of praise for running off the intruder and invited him into the house to guard us while we all went back to sleep. "You saved us," he told Ringo.

The next morning George went into the backyard with the dogs. Ringo meandered with him around to the side of the yard but when he got about twenty feet from the gate, the hair on his back stood up and he ran toward it, barking fiercely just as he had the night before. He could smell where the intruder had been. George went to explore the outside of the gate and saw where the man's shoes had made marks on the gate as he was trying to gain access to our backyard. Whatever his intentions, Ringo's barking had stopped him and driven him off.

CHAPTER EIGHTEEN
Suddenly, Tragically, We Lost Westy.

It seemed a magical day, the day Westy walked into our lives.

We loved terriers, all shapes and sizes. Throughout the years we'd had lots of terriers: a Staffordshire terrier, a Cairn terrier, a couple of mixed-breed terriers, and now Westy.

Smart and independent, the West Highland terrier can also be a little stubborn. They were bred to be tough hunters of vermin and willing to go underground after a fox or badger. They have a tendency to be nuisance barkers and serious diggers. If not well supervised, they will excavate a yard. They require firmness and patience in training. Someone had done a great job with Westy. She was perfectly behaved when she came to us. The vet told us he thought she was about a year old.

Our dog family, at the time Westy joined us, included Kiska, who was half Staffordshire terrier and half Siberian husky; and Cali, our Cairn terrier. We were all happy to welcome Westy to the family. She became the perfect bookend to Cali and a great friend to both Kiska and Cali. She was a happy, loving pup, always welcoming a cuddle or an adventure.

We never knew where Westy came from. When George found her walking on the street, she was well-groomed and well-fed. We tried to find her owner, but none of our efforts bore fruit and so she became ours.

The years passed and so did Kiska and Cali. When Westy was around four years old, we got Ringo and they became a sweet little pack of two.

One winter morning, the damp, soft dirt in our backyard became too tempting for Westy and she started to dig quickly, and with great determination. We watched, only for a moment, before we were able to call her off, but it was too late. Her skillful digging had flung dirt and debris into her face which she had inhaled into her lungs. About a week later, she got a cough and symptoms of great fatigue. When we took her to the vet, Westy was diagnosed with lungs filled with fluid and bacteria, likely from bacterial spores inhaled while digging. There was nothing our vet could do to save her life.

I'm not sure there is anything as heartbreaking as saying goodbye to a beloved dog. Our relationship with our dogs is such an intimate one. They rely on us to meet all their needs. They often sleep with us. They watch over us when we're sick. They amuse us with their playful antics. They are our loyal companions. Loving. Forgiving. They are sources of great joy and the perfect teachers of love. They say that the only bad thing about opening your heart to a dog is that they don't live long enough. I think that's true.

George and I stroked Westy and held her little paws as our vet administered the medication to ease her life away. We talked to her as she faded away; each of us whispering in her ear, telling her what a good girl she was and how much we loved her. We stayed in that room with her body long after her lifeforce had left. We comforted one another through our sobs. We went home without Westy. Ringo's sister was gone.

George and I were devastated, of course. Our precious little pup who had been so full of life and love was suddenly gone. And if anyone ever questions the emotional life of a dog, I challenge you to observe them as they mourn the loss of a loved one. Ringo was confused and depressed by our loss of Westy. He slept a lot more than usual and seemed to be always looking for his sister.

CHAPTER NINETEEN

Matty: Another Sweet Dog Who "Walked" Into Our Lives.

Weeks passed, and Ringo adjusted to Westy being gone. It seemed he didn't mind being an only dog. We kept him busy with mountain biking and agility, lots of frisbee and hikes in the hills. He watched his favorite TV shows and enjoyed long naps in the backyard.

George was settled into this life of having only one dog, and he liked it. He and Ringo could take off anytime they wanted, to go on any adventure they chose. There was a nice sense of freedom they were both enjoying.

One summer evening, July 11th to be exact, George and I were on our way to a friend's home for dinner. As we drove down the main street that connected to our neighborhood, we noticed a little cream-colored dog walking up the sidewalk. We pulled over and as he came running up to us, we saw that his curly hair was so matted that it had formed dreadlocks on part of his body. He was flea-ridden and not neutered. He had no collar or identification of any kind. We couldn't take him with us at just that moment, but we took a long leash from our car and tied him to a tree in a neighbor's front yard. We figured his owner might come by, see him and take him home. If he was still there when we got back, we would take him home with us.

We checked in on our way home and he was there, still tied to the tree. We took him home and scheduled appointments for the vet and the groomer. We decided we would get him all cleaned up, vaccinated, and neutered, then find him a home. He had most likely been living on the streets for quite some time. We wanted to find a loving "forever" home for this sweet boy.

This little guy was a real charmer. He was eager to please. He seemed profoundly happy just to be with us. He loved everything about his new home, especially the food. He loved eating anything and everything. He was a cuddler and a kisser. It seemed he couldn't get enough of expressing his love for us, and receiving ours back. He won Ringo over right away. They played together in the backyard and curled up for naps in the house. Matty was always ready to hop in the car for an adventure and seemed to love our hikes in the canyon just as much as Ringo.

Our plan from the very beginning was not to keep him, but to find him a good home. After a few days I said to George, "Let's give him a name so we can quit calling him Little Guy." It was obvious I was becoming attached to him, so George said back to me, "His name is Temporary." But at about two weeks in, we had all become attached and Ringo really loved his new buddy. George said to Ringo, "Would you like a dog of your own?" And that clinched the deal.

We called him "Matty" and invited him to be a permanent part of our family. We decided that after all he'd been through, he needed a dignified name so he officially became Matthew Patrick. All human kids need a middle name, so parents can invoke the full name when the need arises. It's no different with dogs. For much of the time it's "Awww, Matty, come here, sweetheart." But at times it's, "Matthew Patrick! Stop that digging!" And when there's excitement in the air it might be, "Yay! Matty Patty!! You go Matty!" Matthew loved his home, his family, and ALL of his names.

Ringo and Matty enjoyed a few years as a duo until another misplaced pup entered our lives.

CHAPTER TWENTY

Along Comes Pinto.

George retired from his job in corporate America and was ready to find a way to do some volunteer work in our community. Our neighbor suggested he check out opportunities at our local no-kill animal shelter. He had always been good at training and working with dogs, so volunteering at the shelter, spending time walking and playing with dogs who were waiting for homes was a perfect next step. His work at the shelter opened lots of doors for him and he later apprenticed with the resident dog trainer. His apprenticeship and some further study led George to become a dog trainer himself.

There was one young dog at the shelter named Pinto who became a regular for George. Pinto looked like some kind of mash up of a rat terrier, miniature pinscher and chihuahua. He had an expressive face and a perky body. He was a young dog, under a year old, but had been at the shelter, unadopted for a few months. He was so cute and friendly. We couldn't figure out why he hadn't been adopted.

We started posting photos of him on our Facebook pages, putting out the word that he was a great pup and ready for adoption. Still, no one stepped up, but as our friends read our posts, they would suggest that Pinto was meant to be our dog. We still didn't quite get it.

The animal shelter where Pinto lived hosted a big fundraising event at a local museum. People paid big bucks to attend a comedy event, participate in a silent auction, and make donations to the shelter. A few dogs were selected to be paraded through the social hour right before the show started. Pinto was one of those dogs. Everyone aww'd and oo'd over Pinto but still, no one adopted him.

About a week after the event, George went out to the center to spend another morning playing with Pinto. When he came home, he expressed further frustration that Pinto still had no home. He had learned that Pinto was wrongly housed in the "big dog area" so people who were looking for a little dog never got the opportunity to see him and those who wanted a big dog just passed him by. I finally said what I'd been thinking all along, "Geez, George, why don't you just bring him home? We'll adopt him." And off he went to do the paperwork and bring Pinto home.

There was no adjustment period for the dogs to become bonded to one another. Ringo and Matty readily accepted Pinto into their circle and the pack of two became a family of three.

Pinto loved two things more than anything else in the world: hunting for gophers and sleeping under a blanket. We didn't let him dig for gophers in our yard, but there was a large park-like area we took the dogs to almost every day. He spent plenty of time there with his nose in a number of gopher holes. He actually caught a couple!

We always thought his movements looked very cat-like. When he hunted he would spend several minutes holding perfectly still, staring intensely at the hole where he assumed the gopher to be. Sometimes he would creep closer to the hole, using cat-like paw placement and stealth. And then, at just that perfect moment, he would leap into the air and jump onto the gopher hole, looking much like a cat when hunting a mouse.

Though the smallest of our three dogs, Pinto made certain that he was always the first in line. First to go out the door. First in line for dinner. First to run out of the car and into the park. This little pup seemed to believe he was the biggest, bravest and fastest of them all.

One of Pinto's idiosyncrasies was the way he used his voice. He didn't bark much, but he talked. He made interesting vocalizations that sounded somewhat like a low growl combined with a higher pitched whine. His voice traveled all over the place, sometimes lower tones, sometimes higher, always very expressive and always communicating a need of some kind. Oftentimes, he was asking for a blanket.

We learned to make a blanket available on almost every chair and couch in our living room and family room. If Pinto was home, he wanted to be under a blanket. This was his nirvana. He would hop up on a couch or chair, put his nose under the available blanket, spin his body round and round until he had created a blanket burrito around himself. Then with a big sigh, he'd plop his body down for a long nap. Sometimes, if one of us was sitting right beside him, he would bypass making his own bedroll. He would, instead, nag us to do it for him. He would let out a few whimpers and growls while staring at one of us. This was our cue to toss the blanket over him, tuck it around only slightly and allow him to adjust his body into comfort. We began to call him "the blanket dweller."

George really had a soft spot for Pinto. He was the smallest of our furry family. He had a quirky personality and he began to take up a special place in George's heart.

CHAPTER TWENTY-ONE

And Then There Were Cats.

We've always had at least one dog in our home. For our family, a home wouldn't be complete without a dog. Just as we've always had a dog, I can't remember a time we haven't had a cat or two as well.

When our kids were young, we had two very entertaining Siamese cats: Siddhartha and SukiBuFufu, aka Sidd and Suki. They both lived long, happy lives with our family. Suki went first to the big litter box in the sky right after her fourteenth birthday. Sidd joined her four years later when he was eighteen.

We were so sad after Sidd's passing that we went for quite a few months without a cat's purr in our ears, or a furry body to snuggle up on our laps. We needed time to mourn the loss of our big, goofy boy.

George had adapted nicely to a home with dogs only. He wasn't all that keen on getting another cat. He's always been more of a "dog person" but in living with me for thirty-eight years, he has learned to love cats too. He just wasn't ready to begin litter box duty or take on the job of getting the dogs acclimated to new cats in the house.

Cats are such different creatures than dogs. People often think of all cats as being aloof, arrogant, cranky, but that's because they've never really known a cat. Just like each dog is unique, so is each cat. They have a different way of giving and receiving love.

After about a year, I began to yearn for a kitten. One morning I said to George, "So, listen: I want something and you can't tell me no," and off we went to the animal shelter to pick out a tiny kitten. When we got there, the shelter was overrun with kittens needing homes. We walked through the area where all the kittens were crated, looking into each furry face to try and make a decision about which fur person would go home with us that day.

As we walked by one of the crates, I noticed a litter of three kittens that looked very unique. They had faces like a tabby cat with the typical stripes and swirls of a tabby, but they also had big patches of color on their bodies like the traditional tri-colored calicos. They looked as if they were a mix of the two breeds. I later learned that there is a name for these unique cats. They are called chimeras. A chimera cat is one cat that started out as two. Chimera cats have two sets of DNA because a pair of embryos fused together early in the mother's womb. So, chimera kittens are born with their own individual DNA, plus the DNA from a second embryo.

One of these kittens rushed to the front of her crate as we passed. She stared deeply into my eyes and slowly reached one paw through her crate to touch my face.

She was a gorgeous cat; grey, black, orange, and white in color. Her face held multicolored stripes that looked as though they had been carefully painted on by a thoughtful artist. Her left front leg was made up of bright orange and white horizontal stripes while her right leg displayed the same stripes but in a starkly contrasting black and white. The fur on her body was arranged in a calico pattern of orange, black, white, and grey. The touch of her tiny paw on my face clearly communicated her desire to go home with us.

We chose this kitten, but there were so many who needed homes that I said to George, "We should take two." He agreed and we quickly found our second little girl. She was a traditional grey, white, and peach colored calico.

We each took on the task of naming the kittens. We were both avid cyclists so we chose names that honored that part of our world. We owned several bikes, two of which were single-speed mountain bikes. The model name for George's single-speed was "Solo." That was the name he gave our new chimera girl. I chose the name "Tinker" for the calico. She was named after one of my all-time favorite cross country mountain bike racers, Tinker Juarez.

The kittens were a great fascination for our dogs. At first the dogs chased the cats, but soon enough the cats could hiss and throw a boxing punch like pros. That was enough to keep the dogs in their place and teach them to be courteous with the cats. In no time, they were all friends. The cats joined the dogs for family time on the couch in the evening. During the day, everyone found their favorite place to nap or entertain themselves. Ringo was less than a year old when we got the cats; Matty and Pinto were quite young too. They all grew up together.

CHAPTER TWENTY-TWO
Car Rides Replaced Hikes in the Canyon.

The years moved on, as they do. We were getting older and had lots of great memories to look back on—with kids, grandkids, and all the sweet dogs and cats with whom we'd gotten to share our lives. George and I were in our sixties. Ringo was twelve, Matty nine, and Pinto three. The cats were twelve.

Ringo was beginning to have some trouble getting around. His back knees and hips were causing him to slow down—not because he wanted to, but because ambulation was becoming difficult. He still employed that intense, soulful gaze that said, "Let's go do something fun." If you've ever had a toddler climb into your lap, place their little hands on either side of your face and direct your gaze into their eyes so they could tell you something important, well, that was Ringo. He would place his big head in your lap and stare up into your face with great intensity. The message was clear—either we were running late for his dinnertime or he wanted to be entertained. If we didn't respond immediately, he would give one sharp bark to accentuate his point.

We started him on the vet-recommended anti-inflammatories that might ease his discomfort, and instead of playing frisbee or taking evening walks, we went for drives. We would load the dogs into George's Honda Element and drive around the streets of our neighborhood. We let all the dogs pile into the front seat with us so I, as the passenger, would often have three dogs in my lap: a 50-pound border collie, a 20-pound poodle mix and a 12-pound... well, whatever Pinto was. They would all reach their heads out of the rolled-down passenger window and enjoy a little "car-doggin" as our family called it. It seems like all dogs love car-doggin; hanging their heads out of the windows of a car, taking in the scents as their lips and ears flap a little against the rushing air, squinting their eyes to avoid bugs splatting into their eyes. Pure and simple doggy heaven.

Pinto liked to be on the lookout for bunnies that might be sitting on the side of the road. Matty kept his nose tuned for the smell of food, always his favorite. And Ringo looked for the burros. Yes, burros.

There were packs of wild burros that inhabited the Box Springs Mountain range. Because our neighborhood is at the base of the foothills, we often encountered anywhere from three to 30 burros wandering through our streets. There are places in the U.S. where streets have signs for deer crossings. Our neighborhood has signs for burro crossings.

People were charmed by the burros and would bring carrots and apples in their cars to feed them. Most of the local neighbors knew better than to feed them as it encouraged them to walk up to cars, a danger to them; and graze on our lawns, a nuisance to us. But those who were just driving through the neighborhood would be surprised and intrigued to see burros walking around freely. They would make note of it and come back with kids and grandkids to make an outing of feeding the burros.

Ringo loved the encounters with the burros. Sometimes we would pull the car over to the curb and the burros would come to us, putting their faces right up to, and through, our open windows. Ringo and the burros often got a good face-to-face sniff of each other. They seemed to honor one another's space on this planet. There was plenty of room for dogs, and burros.

CHAPTER TWENTY-THREE
Solo Needs Help.

Ringo was slowing down, and so was Solo. She seemed listless. She was no longer the energetic, athletic cat she had always been. She still followed me from room to room, positioning herself in my lap or on the arm of whatever chair I was sitting in. She loved being close to me, and I adored her. We shared a special connection from the moment we first looked into one another's eyes all those years ago. Even when I was leading a women's wisdom circle or hosting a sacred music evening in our home, Solo was present in my lap, or meandering from guest to guest, making sure everyone felt welcomed.

She was no longer interested in eating much and what she did eat, she often threw up. She was losing weight. It was time to take her to the vet to find out what was going on.

I love our "cat vet"—Riverside Cat Hospital—the only veterinary clinic in our area that catered just to cats. If you've ever taken a cat to the vet, you know they hate sharing space with smelly, old, slobbering dogs. Cats have a finer sensibility about what is civilized and what is not. This clinic was the perfect space for Solo to feel comfortable and relatively at ease about meeting her healthcare professional.

Dr. Leigh is the owner of the clinic and leader of the vet team. She is an angel; patient, kind, never patronizing. She had a solid connection with cats and they seemed to innately trust her. She examined Solo and ordered some blood work that brought the heartbreaking diagnosis of renal failure. Solo's kidneys were failing. Dr. Leigh prescribed two medications. One was an anti-emetic to keep her nausea at bay. The other was a medication that was meant to stimulate her appetite. She also put Solo on a special prescription renal diet and told us to be sure she always had plenty of water. Dr. Leigh explained that a cat with renal failure would likely feel thirsty much of the time.

The combination of these things seemed to help Solo feel better. She started venturing downstairs again, hanging out with the family instead of isolating herself in our bedroom. At night, she kept to her bedtime routine of crawling onto George's chest, going nose-to-nose with him until his breath settled into sleep, and then coming over to snuggle in tightly, right beside my head on the pillow, where she stayed until morning.

Dr. Leigh explained that renal failure is not reversible, but that we could slow it down by managing the symptoms and creating more sustainable nutrition. Once settled into her new health routine, Solo gained some weight and seemed to get most of her energy back. She faced her diagnosis with dignity. She did her best to tolerate the two pills I shoved down her throat every day. But little by little, over the next year, her symptoms worsened. She began throwing up again

I made an appointment to talk with our pet communicator, Amanda, about Solo. My goal was to see if I could get a handle on how to make her more comfortable.

CHAPTER TWENTY-FOUR

How Can We Help Our Solo.

George and I decided to close ourselves into our guest bedroom downstairs to take the call from Amanda. If our fur kids were going to communicate with us, we thought they might like a little privacy. Solo and Tinker were upstairs, asleep on the bed where they usually spent their days. Ringo was resting on the tile floor in the downstairs family room.

The phone rang and we answered to the kind voice of Amanda. We said we wanted to talk with Solo, that she had been having some health issues and we wanted to learn more about her condition and how to help her.

Amanda explained to us that she wanted to connect with Solo and let her have the floor first—to tell us whatever was most on her mind—and after that we could ask Solo any questions we wanted or tell her anything we wanted to tell her. We followed Amanda's lead. She asked if we would give her about three minutes to tune in to Solo, then she would be back to speak with us. For the next three minutes, there was silence on the line.

Here's what Amanda reported to us:

Solo said, "We have lots of animals in our house, but that doesn't matter because I am my mom's favorite, and she knows that she is my favorite. My mom is my favorite thing in the entire world. I want to tell her how divinely connected we are. We've been together in many lifetimes and, in fact, we were sisters in another life."

"My health is declining," she said, "I am just a fraction of what I used to be. Some days I feel okay, like myself again. Other days I'm not feeling good at all. My stomach feels sick all the time. I throw up a lot. Even when I'm

eating, I feel like these little bubbles are bubbling up from my stomach to my chest. My mouth and throat feel dry all the time. I'm parched all the time and I'm always thirsty."

"What she's describing to me sounds like renal failure," Amanda said, "She is showing me such extreme amounts of fatigue. She has pressure, hardness in the part of her body around her kidneys. It feels like there is a big block sitting on that part of her body. She asks that you and George be gentle with her."

"I love being near my mom," Solo continued. "When I'm near my mom, it gives me the feeling like she is grounding me. My mom's energy is very healing to me. She has always been very healing for me, like a dip in the ocean. I just want to be near her. My mom is very intuitive and she knows what I'm going through."

I asked Amanda if she would tell Solo about the pill I had to give her every day to keep her nausea at bay and help her keep her food down. Solo was an elegant cat. I wanted Amanda to tell her that I was sorry for the undignified way I have to get that pill down her throat.

Amanda left the phone again to communicate this to Solo. Here is what she told us when she came back on the line:

"Solo said she knows that you are trying everything to heal her, but she wants you to know that she chose this before she came into her body. She's okay with all of this, even with her physical problems because there is a bigger picture." .

Amanda continued, "My mom's life journey is to be enlightened, not in an ego-based way, but in a way of profound knowing. She has spent so much time and effort to become connected with the divine. She has been doing this her whole life. It's her job, learning how to get closer to Source, closer to The Divine."

Amanda asked Solo if she planned to reincarnate when she left her body. Solo answered, "That's so adolescent! We can connect just as well if I'm not in a body. We will have an even greater connection when I'm in spirit."

I asked Amanda to tell her that I was going to India and will be gone a little over a month. I wanted her to know that George would take good care of her while I was gone.

Solo said, "I already know. My mom goes on these learning vacations. This is her job. I never want her to stop. Of course I'm okay with it. I don't want to do anything to detract from her spiritual growth. Tell her that when she is in India, and when she is in meditation, just to think of me and we'll be connected. She'll know how I'm doing."

"She's such a wise soul. She's such a lady. I think of her like a wise, older Audrey Hepburn," Amanda gushed about our Solo.

Amanda went back to Solo and asked her if there was anything else she wanted to say to us.

"The hard part for my mom and dad about my leaving my physical body is that my brother, their most beloved dog, Ringo, feels like he is getting ready to make his transition too. Neither transition is immediate but they are coming. I want them to be prepared for the aftermath of both me and my brother being gone. Tell my mom she is not connecting with me as deeply as she could. It is so important that she sits with me in meditations. I am here to be her teacher and her guide. I am in my mom's physical space right now. She is caring for me. But after I transition to spirit, she will be in my space and she will be my student."

Amanda said that Solo was an expression of pure love in cat form. She also said that Solo wanted me to know that I didn't need to be sad, that I needed to skip over those mundane emotions because we had bigger things to do.

The time we've scheduled with Amanda was almost done but we wanted to check in briefly with Tinker before we ended our call. I asked Amanda to tell Tinker that I was going to India and will be gone for a month. To that Tinker asked, "She's not going to take the food away is she?" Amanda replied, "No, sweetheart, she's not."

"We all know what's going on. We all know she's going away. Doesn't she know that we're always two steps ahead?" Tinker asked.

With that, we ended our call.

CHAPTER TWENTY-FIVE
Life Goes On.

There is no easy way to prepare for saying goodbye to someone we love. George and I had faced the death of our parents, we'd lost friends and other family members, but let's face it: losing a precious dog or cat is like losing a child. We now had a beloved cat and dog with end-of-life health issues. We knew the time was drawing near and we needed to prepare ourselves for it, but we also needed to do our best to live life to the fullest. We did as much as we could out in nature with Ringo because that's what he loved. And with Solo, there was lots of time spent simply "being." That's what she loved.

During this last year with Ringo and Solo, we also experienced a little health scare with Matty.

We could count on Matty to be the happy little pup that he had always been. Every little thing inspired enthusiastic wagging of his tail. Not only did he seem joyous most of the time, but he was also the epitome of courteousness. He deferred to the other dogs when everyone was in line for a drink. He waited patiently when the back door was opened so that Ringo and Pinto could walk out the door ahead of him. When company came to the house, even though he loved to greet new friends, he waited until everyone else had said their hellos before he went in for a head-scratch or a kind word. He was always the perfect gentleman.

Matty loved to be petted and scratched, so it was routine to rub his belly or scratch his ears when he sat close. As we moved our hands over his warm belly we began to notice little lumps surfacing. They felt kind of soft. They were moveable under the skin. It started with one or two but soon there were about six. One had grown to the size of a small golf ball.

We knew of other dogs who had experienced these lumps. Usually they were lipomas, fatty tumors. But sometimes they turned out to be cancer.

We scheduled a vet visit for Matty. We wanted to make sure we weren't facing cancer. Our vet did an aspiration biopsy on two of the lumps. It turned out that there was no clear indication of cancer. They appeared to be lipomas, nothing to worry about, but we couldn't be absolutely sure unless we had them all removed and sent to pathology for a more conclusive biopsy. Matty was due for a teeth cleaning and, while under anesthesia, the vet could easily remove the tumors, do a further biopsy, and make sure they were all benign. We decided to schedule the surgery.

We had been through a previous trauma with Matty that caused us to fear we would lose him. As we waited for him to awaken from this surgery, and then endure the long wait for the biopsy results to come back, we couldn't help but call to mind how frightened we had been all those years ago.

Matty was about three years old when we were doing a brisk night hike in Sycamore Canyon. The moon was bright, the coyotes were singing, it felt like we were the only people on earth. Ringo and Matty were off lead, enjoying the freedom of running a little ahead of us to search for interesting smells and give chase to the brave Kangaroo Rats that held their station, even upon the appearance of a miscreant dog. All of a sudden, a German Shepherd appeared on the trail. His peeps were with him but he, too, was off lead. He and Matty ran into one another and the Shepherd grabbed Matty, shook him a bit and tossed him to the side of the trail. It all happened very quickly and was pretty terrifying.

We made a trip to the emergency clinic to have Matty's wounds treated. A few stitches and some bandages seemed to make him whole again, but two days later, he suddenly became paralyzed in his hind legs. He couldn't stand, he couldn't walk, and as he made certain movements he cried out in pain.

We took him back to our vet. After x-rays and examination, our vet told us we had a severely injured dog. The encounter with the shepherd had caused a spinal injury that was delayed in showing itself. It was clear now that Matty had suffered damage to his spine. Our only choices were to be referred to a canine spine specialist, who would do a very expensive surgery and rehabilitation protocol that may or may not be successful, or euthanize our sweet Matty!

We went home with some pain medication and a heavy heart. What would we do?

I became obsessed with finding a way to help Matty. I called our agility trainers. They had three Shetland Sheepdogs who were elite athletes. Nancy and Kay had a cadre of professionals to care for their dogs: acupuncturists, chiropractors, psychologists, psychics.

I called Nancy, crying, "Sob, sob, sob, Nancy, sob, sob, the vet says we should put Matty to sleep, sob, sob. He injured his spine. Can't walk. He's in pain, sob, sob."

In perfect "Nancy form" she said to me, "Kathy, get ahold of yourself, right now!! Write this number down. It's Jacqueline De Grasse. She is our chiropractor. She will help Matty. He'll be fine."

I called Dr. De Grasse and told her the story. She said she needed an x-ray so she could see where the injury was, and that Matty needed to get a steroid shot so the inflammation would go down and she could manipulate his spine without hurting him too badly. She called the vet she routinely worked with and got us in immediately. Matty had his x-ray, got his shot, and we were off to see Dr. De Grasse.

The clinic was in a small home-turned-chiropractor's office, but unlike other chiropractor offices, this waiting room was filled with dogs and cats. As we sat in the room awaiting our turn, the people who were there with their pets were eager to tell us stories of how Dr. De Grasse had saved their pet. We heard story after story of miraculous healing.

"My cat had a broken spine. They said she'd never walk again. Now she's fine."

"My dog was hit by a truck. The vet said he needed to be put to sleep. He's running around now like nothing happened."

George and I were told so many tales of complete recovery that a cautious brand of hope was instilled in our fearful hearts.

It was Matty's turn to be seen. Dr. De Grasses greeted him with a loving hand and a generous heart. She spoke so sweetly to him that it almost made me weep. She was a small woman with eyes that told you she knew things that were beyond knowing. She gently felt the length of his spine, walked from top of neck to base of tail with her strong hands, manipulating each of the vertebrae. She said that, though the problem was manifesting itself in the bottom of his spine, the injury that was causing the problem was actually in his neck. She then employed George to hold Matty firmly between his hands, at Matty's shoulders, as she gave him traction by pulling back strongly at the base of his tail.

When her treatment was complete, she gave us a homeopathic anti-inflammatory we were to give him four times a day. She also instructed us to purchase a pediatric enema from our drug store to clear what, on x-ray, looked like some impacted fecal material. She told us to take him home and let him rest, to call her the following morning and tell her how he was doing.

Matty slept well through the night. We didn't. We tossed and turned with worry for our little guy. We couldn't wait for that long night to be over, to see how he would be doing the next day. We hurried down the stairs in the morning, and were greeted by a wagging tail! The enthusiastic wag that was so characteristic of Matty had gone missing for almost two weeks. Boy was it great to see him being waggy again. We put him carefully into the sling we'd been using to move him around, and took him outside to go potty.

George walked him slowly across the yard and soon called out excitedly, "He's weight-bearing, Kath." George continued to gently guide him and soon Matty was walking on his own. He walked all around the yard, of his own volition. We were thrilled and we both began to cry.

We took Matty back for all the prescribed follow-up visits with Dr. De Grasse. He got stronger with each adjustment and was soon running and jumping like nothing had ever gone wrong.

Earlier in these pages, I introduced Amanda as a miracle in our lives. Well, Jacquie De Grasse is another miracle. I feel like George and I have met two bonafide angels because of our dogs. We're so grateful to have these angels on our team.

Now we were waiting for the results of Matty's biopsy, hoping some angels would intervene once again and give us good news. Please, please tell us that these lumps are not cancer.

After a week of waiting for a pathology report, we were finally home free. Matty had no cancer. The lumps which were just fatty tumors were not dangerous and, in fact, were now gone.

CHAPTER TWENTY-SIX

It's Time to Talk to Matty.

We'd spoken to Ringo and Solo through the *miracle of Amanda*. It was time to talk with Matty.

The phone rang, and we answered to hear Amanda's sweet voice. She asked if we were still planning on talking with Matty on her call. We said yes and she said she wanted to take a moment to tune into his energy and learn what he wanted to say, then we could ask questions or tell her anything that we'd like to share with him.

She placed us on hold for about three minutes then came back on the line to tell us this:

"Matty is a really interesting little fellow. I asked him if he wanted to tell me about how he felt about life and about being with you guys and just what he wanted to share," she said,

"The first thing I want to say is that if there is just one word that I would use to describe him it would be either happy or optimistic. He seems to be an eternal optimist. He's a real don't-worry-everything-is-going-to-work-out kind of guy."

Amanda said that she asked, "Have you always had that attitude, because from your parents' description, you had a rough beginning."

"No, I never had a rough beginning," he said. "It wasn't that bad. I was really always focused and always intentional about where I was heading."

Amanda said, "Okay, meaning what? What does that mean?"

"I always knew where I was going to go and it's where I am now. I knew that the road that I took had to be the road that led me to where I belong."

"I understand that," Amanda replied. "So, even in the beginning you had a pretty optimistic attitude?"

"I wouldn't say it was optimistic, I would say it was certain. My life is really good and I'm really happy," Matty answered.

"So tell me a little bit about yourself," Amanda continued. "Your parents would like to get to know you on a deeper level, so how can I help them do that?"

Amanda shared with us what Matty told her then, "The first thing he wants to say is how much he appreciates that you always treat him like he's a kid and not like your pet."

"They even have birthdays for me and I appreciate that so much. I feel like I'm just a child," Matty told Amanda.

Amanda asked him, "How about your health? Do you feel like you're in pretty good health?" And he said "Yes, why are you asking?"

"Well, because I don't know your age and I was wondering if you wanted to tell me how old you are and also when I'm connecting with you, I'm feeling a little bit of something like muscle tenderness and if you were four, that would concern me. If you were ten, it wouldn't. So, can you tell me a little bit about your health and how old you are?"

"Yeah, where do you want me to start?"

"Start at the beginning. Start with your health, let's talk about that," Amanda asked him.

"I feel good. I thought that I was going to be leaving not too long ago, maybe a few years or so ago."

"How come?" Amanda asked.

Matty told her that he felt like there was a lot of worry and a lot of concern and his body felt very lumpy.

"But you're OK now?" She asked.

"Yes, I'm OK. It was nothing. My body was just lumpy."

"But you're OK now?"

"Yeah, how come you keep asking?"

"Because that's a really big thing for a human to hear," Amanda told him. "Did you have anything that you know of?"

"No, but it wasn't cancer, it wasn't cancer, it wasn't cancer and that was the celebration. It wasn't cancer."

"And you feel good in your body now?"

"Yeah, I don't have cancer in my body and I will never have it."

"OK, good. But what is this muscle soreness or tightness that I'm feeling from you around your neck and shoulders, do you have that a lot?" she asked.

"Yeah, I have that a lot."

"Is there anything we can do about it?"

"No, but it feels really good when my mom heals me. She's really good at healing."

"How about your dad?" Amanda asked.

"He's not as good as my mom, but he's good too."

"How would you like them to heal you? Literally heal you?" she asked. "Take you to the vet? What do you mean?"

"No, just put their hands on me. I'm going to give you an analogy of how it feels. If I had a sunburn and someone just rubbed a little bit of yogurt or aloe on my skin, it just feels really, really good."

"Okay, so the muscle tenderness, there's nothing associated with that, it's just age?" she asked him.

"Yes, it's just muscle tenderness and it feels better when my mom puts her hands on me. She heals me."

Amanda told us: "Matty's discomfort is not like muscle pain, but just like if I went on a really long car ride and I feel like I have to stretch the kinks out. He feels that a lot, but only through his neck to his shoulder blades and it stops right around his ribs. So, it's not the back. It's the front part of his body where he feels the tightness and the muscle soreness. It's not concerning, it's barely painful, but it's just something I want to mention. Nothing major, just muscle tenderness but putting your hands on him feels like a release and makes him feel so much better."

Amanda continued, "Now, I'm going to ask him about his life, what he likes, any pet peeves that he has."

She left the phone for a few minutes then came back to us. "Matty is so interesting. As much as I feel like when I connect to him he's very happy and sweet and I just get a very loving, affectionate dog; when I connect longer with him, I have to say that there is a real depth underneath that bubbly exterior. He really is an old soul. It's a little bit harder to see with him because he's just so happy and so loving that upon first connection I guess I didn't realize how really deep he was."

"Matty, tell me about the things that you love?" Amanda asked him. "He said, 'Okay.' So, I asked if he has any pet peeves. He said, 'Pet peeves?' Well, this won't take long because there is not much to go over, but I want to tell you a little bit more about me. Can you get to know me more?'"

"Of course, I can get to know you," Amanda told him.

Matty then told Amanda, "Okay, well did you know that I love loving?" And Amanda said, "Yes, I figured that out."

"Can you tell my parents how much my favorite thing to do, well, one of my favorite things to do, is love like oh, kiss and love and just be in love and kiss." And he said, "I would love to just be romantic."

"What does romantic mean to you?" she asked him.

"Just let me kiss you, just let me love you, just let me admire you. If I could write poetry, I would write poetry. If I could just listen to music and write poetry, I would do both of those things," he said. "So, can you tell them that?"

And then he said, "And I love the smell of food cooking. Well, I love food, even if it's not cooking. I love any kind of food, even if it's disgusting." He showed Amanda a very clear image of a cat. And she said, "Cat food?", "Yeah, cat food but . . . "

"Cat poop?" she asked.

"Well, if I could I would. I know I shouldn't, but it is so appealing to me," he said. "I do everything with passion. I do everything with all my heart. Whether that's eat, or whether that's love, or whether that's be in the moment, I do everything with all of it."

Amanda tells us that he's describing that he's not a little in or a little out. When he is focused, he's completely intense like he's all in.

"And that's one of my favorite things about me, how much I give. Like when I love, I just love with all of my heart and when I want something I want it so bad, so passionately," Matty told her.

"I have really pleading eyes." He said that he felt that when he speaks with his eyes he speaks volumes; that his eyes are like reading a novel when you look into them. That's how he feels about himself. And I said, "Honey, you know, I'll be honest with you. You talk a lot in poetry when I'm talking to you. What does that mean to you?" And he told me, "That's just how I think."

"If Matty were human and he were able to explain something, he would explain it in a way that sounded very poetic, very artistic, and very beautiful, very soft, and very graceful. That's how he would talk. He sees himself as being more complex in his thought pattern but having that softness and that poetry about himself. And that's something that's really important to him, and it's something that he really wants you two to understand about him, that he has this gentleness about him."

She explained, "I want to describe him to you as if he were a human. If he were a human, this is what he would look like: He would have long hair and he would keep it in a man bun and he would be dressed in converse and jeans and a blazer. He would look casual, but like he could possibly teach art history classes. That's how he would present himself. This is what he sees as a portrayal of how he would look and how he would think. Sometimes animals show me what they would look like as a human, and I see them in that way because that shows me a lot of how they want to be known as a dog or who they are on the inside. The reason I'm describing what Matty looks like, his version of himself, is so that you can see a different side of him."

Amanda continued. "I asked him to tell me more about his life, but to keep it really simple. He said, 'Well, I can't really keep it simple because I'm not real simple.' 'Yes, I'm noticing that about you,' I told him. Then he said, 'I'm not a show off.' He says he likes to be lowkey. So, I asked him what he meant by lowkey and again, he showed me this image of this man. Like you would look at this man with a man bun, very good looking, fair, blue eyes, very attractive. Maybe hasn't shaved for about a day, so he has a slight little bit of facial hair and the blazer and the jeans and the converse. You would look at him and you wouldn't really think he is as intelligent as he is, but he would have an extremely high IQ as a person. But you would look at him, and the way he presents himself isn't someone who looks cocky, or presents as, 'I'm so much smarter than you and I'm so much better than you and I have this great job'. He has this humbleness and this down to earth-ness. He could have a conversation with someone who is homeless and he could have a conversation with an astronaut."

Amanda asked him why he was sending her this image of this man.

"Because that's who I am in dog form," was his answer. He said he felt that he was really respectful and didn't want to show off his high intelligence and make others feel like they're beneath him, even though mentally that might be the case. "But you know I'm not rude, so I'm not a show off because being a show off is rude," he said.

"I asked that he tell me some of his favorite things and he said, 'Everything that I've been telling you is my favorite thing. Loving is my favorite thing; treats, snacks, those are my favorite things, and being respectful and being this artistic gentleman, these are my favorite things. This is what life is all about.'"

Amanda then asked him, "Do you want to tell me some of your pet peeves?"

"Well, I have only really one pet peeve. I don't like to be told no, that I can't have something."

"What is that thing that you can't have that you would really want?" she asked.

"Well, snacks. But I'm real respectful about it. I don't like it, but I'm still respectful about it."

Matty had more to say, "Can I tell you something about my life and something I didn't like?" He told Amanda that the event that forced him to leave his prior home was 4th of July fireworks. That, for him, was the exit. It was the grand finale of why it was time to leave where he was. He said, "And that was that. I bolted. I shot out of there. For me, those sounds and the air and those fireworks and all of the explosions, that was the Universe's gift to me of giving me a way out. I mean, I was able to leave somewhere without it like being a big deal or anyone noticing or anyone caring."

"Do you want to tell me what your life was like before you left?" Amanda asked.

"A lot of neglect, outside, unimportant, dry, desert. I wasn't treated like anything other than a dog that was left in the garage. If there was any shelter at all, it was miniscule. It wasn't even like a garage; it was more like a carport," he said. "There was never love. There was never affection. There was never a 'we're so happy to have you, you're such a wonderful dog', it was more like 'oh, I think I'll remember to throw out food, but I might not'. And it wasn't specifically dog food. It was whatever was on hand, whatever they remembered to put out."

He continued, "I knew that my life was destined for so much more. I knew where I was meant to go. As soon as I heard those explosions in the sky, that was the Universe telling me, 'Okay, today is the time to leave.'"

"So, the 4th of July is significant for you?"

"Yes, that was the day that I left where I didn't belong any longer. And did you know that 4th of July is my mom's birthday?" he asked. "I knew where I was going. It was very intentional and all I saw was like a lighthouse."

Amanda then told us, "That's how looking at your energies was for him. It was like a big light in the dark, and he just followed that light. And he followed that light, and he followed that light. He didn't know how to get there as far as take a turn here, go this way. He was just following a light in the dark."

"Was it literally dark outside or are you being figurative?" Amanda asked him.

"No, I'm being figurative. Do you understand that? Do you understand that where I lived was dark and awful, and then I experienced this (and he showed her all these explosions in the sky), and then I heard the angels say, 'now is the time, let's go.'"

"He said as he was journeying to your house, all that he saw was this beacon of light and he followed that beacon of light. He said it took him one week, from July 4th to July 11th."

"Okay, I got it," Amanda said, "What was that beacon of light symbolic of?"

"My family. It was guiding me to where I belong, my soul purpose, being at home." He said that also after he got to where he belonged, it was very instant and everybody knew that it was where he was supposed to be, where he belonged. It was just an energetic knowing. An intuition.

"I'm so thankful that I'm okay because there was a time I questioned how long I was going to stay," he said.

Amanda asked, "Because you had some lumps or something?" And he answered, "No, because I didn't think I was ever going to be able to walk again. But that taught my parents the power of thought and intention. That was a powerful moment where intention meant everything. There was nothing that a doctor could say or do that intention didn't prove. Everybody thought it was completely impossible that I would walk again, but intention proved it was possible. When my parents took me to the lady that pushed on my back and we all had the intention that I would get better, then it happened."

"Not to be rude, but what is the point of you telling me this?" Amanda asked.

"The point is, because I came into this life to teach them about intention and I feel like I have done that."

Matty went on to say, "If I could say three things to describe what my journey is I'd say happiness, love, affection, that is number one. Number two is to just enjoy the moment and be respectful. And number three is this: If I could really sum up what's important to me in this lifetime it's teaching them the importance of intention and just trusting that everything is going to be okay even when it feels like it's not. That's what I came here to do and I feel like I'm doing a really stellar job of that. I want them to know how much I love them and how powerful this journey is that we're sharing together. I want them to know that every step of the way, even when things seemed like they weren't okay, they were always okay and it was just my job to teach them that intention is everything."

And then he added, "Food is really delicious, and that is part of enjoying this life and enjoying being in a physical experience. Being in a spiritual, non-physical body is wonderful, but one of the absolute joys we have in this life is eating because it's something we can't experience when we're in a non-physical body. But it's not just eating, it's a variety of snacking. It's trying different things; It's trying different foods. So, can you tell them that a buffet is important to me, even if it's one tiny little bite of something different. That's one of the experiences I came here to enjoy."

"He wants you to know that if there is anything that you can give him that would make his life better, it would be a little tiny piece of sushi or hamburger or something like that because the experience of tasting different flavors and textures is one of the real joys of being in a physical body," Amanda said.

"And he prefers to be called Matthew. He feels it is more dignified and better represents who he is."

And that ended our call.

CHAPTER TWENTY-SEVEN

We Were Blown Away.

We were blown away by the accuracy of everything Amanda told us about her conversation with Matthew. Yes, he was our courteous dog. Yes, he appeared to always be joyful, no matter the circumstance. Yes, he loved to eat—anything and everything. In fact, we needed to keep a careful eye on his weight. His well-developed doggy physique could easily slip over the line into a "portly short" if we were not careful. Yes, he was a lover; always kissing, snuggling close, enjoying lap time and massage time.

Her description of the stories of his challenges also hit right on the nose. The lumps on his torso, the fear that it might be cancer. The paralysis and suggestion that he might never walk again, or might not even make it through this terrible injury. His ultimate healing and his ability to walk again. It was amazing to us that all of this was accurate and that Amanda was able to so fully tune in to Matthew's history.

My most favorite part of Matthew's story was his telling of the Fourth of July when he was guided by the Universe to leave his meager dwelling and seek his destiny, to find his soul family. He left on July 4th as the Universe was exploding with the vibration of noise and color and followed the bright light that led him to us one week later. It was July 11th, exactly one week after my Independence Day birthday when we found him walking up the street and into our arms.

Because of our phone call with Amanda, we now had a new perspective about Matthew. We felt like we knew him with a greater depth of understanding than we ever had before. We now recognized him as the intelligent, dignified being that he was.

We decided it was time to make an appointment to talk with Pinto.

CHAPTER TWENTY-EIGHT
Pinto, "The Potty Mouth" Talks to Amanda.

After the cursory hellos, Amanda got right to it and connected with Pinto. Here is what she said:

"So, he is funny. He is very different. Sorry, I'm laughing but he's so funny. The way that I see Matty is this possible art director or literature professor. It is the absolute and complete utter opposite of how I see Pinto. I don't even know where to start this conversation. Sorry, it just really took me by surprise how different he is. I said, 'Pinto, tell me a little bit about your life and, are you happy?' He said, 'First of all, I want to talk about why the fuck don't they celebrate my birthday the way they celebrate his (Matty)? With his, it is like a full all-out celebration and with mine it's like, oh it's... what's the date? Sept 26, Sept 27, Sept 28, Sept 29, oh, it's October already, oh we totally fucking forgot about Pinto.'"

Amanda tried to contain her laughter and continued, "Oh, honey, that's so much bad language. Do you always talk like that?"

"Fuck yeah, I always talk like that," he told her.

"Wow! Okay, that is a lot of bad language."

"How else am I supposed to talk?"

"Well, maybe you could just leave out some of the 'f' words."

"Oh, shit. Okay, I'll try."

She asked him if he always talked like that and he answered, "Yeah, I do."

"Okay, I got it," was her reply.

"He was very sassy," she said. "You have a pretty sassy personality."

"Well, listen, I came here to kick ass. I'm not really accomplishing that yet, but that is actually my goal," he told her.

"Kick ass like what?" she asked.

"Well, look at me."

She said, "'Show me how you see yourself. How do you perceive yourself?' He showed me himself as this giant, strikingly beautiful, black panther. Muscles rippling, claws out, big fangs, ready to hunt and kill and prowl, like this fierce, big, beautiful animal. And I said, 'You know that you don't look like that, right?'"

"Yeah, I know!! Fuck, I know!! But in my mind, I do," he told her. "In my mind, the second I close my eyes I become this. I'm much more primal than the others and that's what I love about myself. You want to talk about things I love? I fucking love that about myself."

"I'll be honest, I'm going to have a really hard time relaying all these words. Should I just say it the way I'm receiving it?" she asked him.

"Fuck, yeah. Can you tell them how much I love being this big scary beast? Do they know that I really look like this?"

"No, I don't think they know."

"I was supposed to be like a Rottweiler, or a Pitbull, then I said, no, no, I know, I want to be a Doberman. I had that image in my mind, it was so clear and the next thing I know, I stopped growing and I'm like, fuck! I'm not a Doberman."

"No, you're not," she said.

"But I thought I was so clear."

"I'm sorry, honey. Maybe it wasn't supposed to be part of your path or maybe you just flubbed the intention a little."

"Fuck yeah, I did. I mean I wouldn't be here if I was a big scary Doberman though."

"No, you probably wouldn't," she agreed with him.

"But I am in my mind, tell them that."

"Okay, I got it. I'll tell them that." Amanda said.

"I wish I was a cat sometimes," he continued.

"You wish you were a cat? I was not expecting that. How come you wish you were a cat?"

"Because cats do so many things that I wish I could do. They can jump, they can climb trees, they can hunt, they can kill, they can chase. They're very sleek and very stealth."

"Pinto is not that, of course, but he wished he was. And so, in his mind he perceives himself to be not like a mountain lion or a wolf or that kind of hunter, but a very specific big, giant black cat. So, I said to him, 'I got it. I understand, you're a panther.'"

And he said, "Can you tell them how much I want that? I love the idea of it. I fucking love it. I talk about it constantly with my brothers. I always make pictures that say, hey, wouldn't it be cool one day to be a cat? And everyone else says, well, no, yeah, well maybe, I guess it would have its ups *and downs. But I'm like, hey, think of all the cool things we could do if we were a cat. Everyone else is less in awe of it than me."*

"So, Pinto has a mouth of a sailor. And the one thing he wants to complain about more than anything else is why do you always forget his 'f-ing' birthday?!?'" Amanda said.

"We don't actually know his birthday. We adopted him from a shelter," George explained to Amanda.

"Well, Pinto says it is sometime in September. The day that he came into your life, was it around that time?"

We told Amanda that we weren't sure, but that we have a record of the date in our file.

"Well, you should probably celebrate it around that time because for him Sept 19 or 29 is significant. I don't mean to say that he's really immature, but he is very, very different. I feel like he's a much younger soul. He doesn't have the depth. There was such a selfless energy that I was getting from Matt and Ringo. With Pinto it's much more instant gratification and in the now and more self-serving energy," she told us.

"I asked Pinto if there was anything he dislikes," Amanda continued. "And he said, 'Yes, really I dislike that my brother, Matty, always says, 'Excuse me, my name isn't Matty, it's Matthew. Excuse me, can you call me Matthew, I really prefer to go by Matthew. Would you mind calling me Matthew?' I do mind."

Apparently, in Pinto's mind, Matty is always wearing sweaters, she tells us.

"'So, Matty enjoys wearing sweaters?' I asked him. Pinto said, 'No, he looks like that, he looks like that, he looks like he's always wearing sweaters.'"

"Okay, so in his mind he's wearing sweaters or in real life?" Amanda asked him.

And he said, "Well, I wear clothes sometimes, only it's different."

"Why is it different?" she asked.

"Because I don't have a choice, but in Matty's mind, he always has on sweaters. More specifically, turtle necks, and even more specifically red. And he's always wearing them in his mind. Then he says, 'Would you mind calling me Matthew instead of Matty? I really am kind of old for Matty. I'm an adult now. Would you mind calling me Matthew?' he says that all the time. He's sooo annoying. And his idea of always being polite, well he comes off more annoying than polite. There's nothing wrong with being an asshole sometimes," Pinto said.

"You want something? Everyone needs to move out of the way and I'll get what I want. There is nothing wrong with wanting to be first in line, there's nothing wrong with wanting that," he told Amanda.

"No, there's not. There's nothing wrong with wanting that."

"But, the way I go about it, is that wrong?" he asked Amanda.

"So, you think you're pushy?" she replied.

"Yeah, I'm pushy."

"Um, no, that's just you. There's nothing wrong, it's just you," she told him.

"Matty's not like that and that's just so annoying to me. He always has to be such a Mr. Good Guy, Mr. Goody Two Shoes," he said. "I don't want to be Mr. Goody Two Shoes. I don't aspire to be that."

"You know we're really getting off topic here. Do you want to tell me some of your favorite things? How about we talk about some of the things that you really love?" Amanda changed the subject.

"I will tell you what I don't like. I don't like when I don't get my way and when my brother is always being polite. It is so annoying. Matty would be obese if he could, but he has a good metabolism anyway so he wouldn't be, but he would be. I don't get the big obsession with food."

"Well, it sounds like your obsession with hunting or the idea of hunting is like his obsession with food. The same, right? Both your greatest loves?"

"Yeah, I guess you could say that," he agreed.

Amanda then asked, "Do you want to tell me about some of the other things that you like or anything that you don't like?"

"I love going outside. I love doing things. I love being active. I love—hey what's on the agenda for today? Are we going to do anything today? Can we go anywhere? It's kind of boring in here. How about, hey, let's go outside. Let's see what's going on. Hey, do you want to go for a hike? Hey, let's go for a walk. Hey, let's have an adventure. Hey, let's do something. I really like to be going and I really like to be doing. I really, really like that a lot."

He continued, "But when I'm in the house, I like to be warm. I like to be comfortable. I get cold pretty easily and that's why I don't really mind wearing clothes, wearing sweaters, because I do get cold and I like the warmth of sitting on somebody's lap, not because I want the affection but because I want the body heat."

"Well, that's pretty rude, but I'll tell them that," Amanda said.

"That's OK, they won't mind. They'll understand," he said, "I don't like how cold I get so fast. It's so annoying. Actually the bottom of my feet."

"Your feet get cold or your legs?"

"My legs, but especially my feet. My feet get so cold."

"Okay, anything else you want to talk about that you love, or don't love?" she asked again.

"Well, I like spending time with my oldest brother. I really enjoy his company. Whereas Matthew rubs me the wrong way sometimes because I think he thinks he's better than me, and it's just because his mind is very complicated and I get real focused on one thing. I always like adventure and I enjoy like the hunt of life and he likes to think. He's a thinker. I don't like to think all the time. So, I enjoy the company of my older brother more because he's not so obnoxious. He also likes the idea when I pitch to him about being a cat."

Amanda said to us, "I usually don't like to ask people questions, but did I tell you that your older dog was considering being a cat?"

"Yes," I replied.

"This is where it's extending from because Pinto is obsessed. Let me repeat this: Pinto is obsessed with the idea of being a cat so he can hunt and jump and pounce and be stealth and smooth and lots of things that he's not in this little body of his. And so, because he talks about it all the time and he's pitching the idea, sure it does sound like it would be kind of appealing to his brother, Ringo. That's where it's coming from. He won't stop talking about it. Like every other image he takes me back to how cool it would be to be a cat because he could bring in dead lizards. How cool would it be to be a cat, bring in these gophers. How cool would it be to be a cat. He would bring in chipmunks. It's really all about the hunting and being able to go outside and do things because those are things that he really loves. He loves adventure. He loves being outside. He loves the smell of fresh air. He loves the feeling of the wilderness, which is so funny because he is so little, but in his mind he is not." She stopped and took a breath.

"His communication to me is so interesting because it's so young. He is such a young soul. He's not as domesticated as many other dogs, specifically your other dogs. He's much more, well, he calls himself primal.

"The things that he loves are hunting, nature, adventure, going out for walks, going places, doing things, and sitting on someone's lap for warmth. Anything warm. I feel if he could drink warm tea he would. He likes the idea of not being cold. As soon as he gets cold it's very uncomfortable for him very fast. Heat doesn't bother him the way the cold does. In fact, he loves the heat. He loves feeling like he's going outside to have a hunting and fishing expedition. He loves the great outdoors.

"One thing he doesn't like about being a dog is barking, so he makes these more internal sounds as though he is still a different animal. Like you wouldn't hear a hunting bird barking. You would hear them making cawing sounds or a more internal vocal sound, and you also wouldn't hear a cat barking. You would maybe hear them purr or make an internal meow sound and that's how he likes to vocalize." (We told Amanda, that's absolutely true, he does it all the time.) "Yes," she said, "It's because he doesn't really dislike being a dog, but he's really hung up on the cat hunting thing.

"He really has a lot of affection and love and respect and admiration for your oldest dog, Ringo. I don't want to say that he doesn't like Matthew, but he is definitely his least favorite out of every one.

"Also, back to Matthew for a moment, he said that if we could call him Matthew sometimes he would really like that. It makes him feel very mature, very grown up. He really enjoys that.

"As far as Pinto's health goes, he feels excellent to me. I'm not feeling any discomfort in his body at all except for his extreme aversion to cold. If it's under 72 degrees, all of a sudden he's like, oh my god it's freezing in here, someone turn up the fucking heat, someone cover me with a blanket or put a sweater on me. And so for him, he has an extreme aversion to anything less than warm."

CHAPTER TWENTY-NINE

Yep. That's Our Little Blanket Dweller.

We learned so much about Pinto during this conversation with Amanda. We already knew that he loved being under a blanket. In fact, we nicknamed him the blanket dweller. He does get cold and shivers easily. His favorite place in the whole world is on a couch under a blanket, even during hotter-than-hot Southern California heat. If we go out for a walk, when it's even a little cold outside, he wants a sweater to keep him warm. If we're sitting on a couch without a blanket, he will sit next to us and make small cries until someone gets up to get him a blanket. He then twirls around, pulling the blanket around him until he has wrapped himself into a blanket burrito. Then, he is happy.

What about his hunter tendencies?

We take all the dogs, almost daily, to a park area near our home so they can have a little time to run free. It's a large, grassy, fenced-in area. No other dogs there—only us. There are lots of gopher holes in the park inviting Pinto to be the great hunter he imagines himself to be. As the other dogs run and chase, he busies himself hunting gophers.

When Pinto told Amanda he sees himself as a big, beautiful black panther, we could totally see how he has that vision of himself. When he walks on to the expansive carpet of grass, he creeps along very purposefully—not doglike at all—but slowly and stealthily, just like a cat. As he nears a hole that looks promising, he lifts his front feet, arches his back, and pounces like a cat would. He will stare into a hole with unswerving intensity and make little internal sounds in his throat never barking, just uttering a cross between a whine and a whispered growl. He spends a good amount of time with his snout pushed down into the hole, inhaling the scent, listening for movement under the ground and waiting until the time is right to dig and pounce again. On occasion, he actually has caught and killed a gopher. More often than not, he works his way around the big area of lawn, going from hole to hole, performing all the duties of the perfect hunter. Black panther, indeed. He has earned the right to this vision.

The thing that was somewhat shocking to us was his rather immature, self-centered personality and his potty mouth. Wow, could he use the f-bomb! We knew that he always pushed his way to the front of the line whenever we were going out into the backyard, getting loaded up into the car, or going through the gate at the park. It was true—he always wanted to be first. But his disgust with the fact that we hadn't celebrated his "f-ing birthday" was a big surprise.

As George told Amanda, we didn't know when his birthday was and we weren't even sure of the date that we adopted him. Pinto told Amanda the dates that were important to him: September 19 and September 29. She suggested we choose one of those dates to celebrate his birthday.

When the call was over, we went to our pet records right away. We wanted to know what his adoption date was. We fingered our way through the files where we kept all the information about vet appointments, immunization records, adoption certificates, and the likes. When we looked into Pinto's file, sure enough, we adopted him on September 19th! That would now always be the date we celebrate his birthday.

CHAPTER THIRTY

"The Park" Becomes Ours.

The sweet rhythm of routine allowed for relative order in our home. With three dogs and two cats, one would think that chaos could easily ensue, but it did not.

Everyone loved each other—humans, dogs, and cats. At night, all the dogs were happily crated for sleep. Though we had three crates, Matty and Pinto preferred snuggling up together in one crate. Ringo held real estate in the large crate positioned next to theirs. Solo and Tinker slept on the bed with us; Solo choosing the pillow next to my head, and Tinker staying close to George.

In the morning, after everyone had breakfast, we took the dogs to "The Park" to play.

The Park is a large fenced-in area of grass, baseball field, picnic tables, bar-b-que pits, benches, and a fire pit, appointed by three giant pepper trees. It was actually the recreation area of the Mormon Church and was just around the corner from our home. We could see The Park from our home by simply stepping out our front door. The bishop of the church generously let us exercise our dogs in this expansive area.

This was doggy heaven. There are not many places in our town where dogs can simply be, without restraint, allowed to follow their own instincts. Yes, there are dog parks, but those aren't always a very safe bet. The only downside to The Park was that other people brought their dogs to play here as well. Not many, but enough that we had to be on the lookout for someone coming through the gate and not shutting it behind, or bringing an aggressive dog and letting it off lead. And it seemed we were always picking up dog poop, not just our dogs' poop, but all the other dogs' poop as well. Sometimes it seemed like no one was cleaning up but us. And it's a little like when you have kids. You don't mind changing your own kid's diaper, but someone else's kid's dirty diaper just might cause you to gag. Sometimes there were fast-food wrappers and plastic cups tossed about. We cleaned those up too. We took all this in stride because we felt so grateful for being able to use this beautiful space.

After a year or so, the bishop felt the need to make some changes. He let us know that miscreant teenagers and some homeless folks were using the park and leaving big messes behind. This wasn't news to us. We had been cleaning up their messes. He was going to have to put a lock on the gate to keep everyone out, *everyone but us*. The bishop had been grateful for the way we had always kept an eye on the park, letting him know when there was something amiss. A water leak, a broken sprinkler, people using the area for a late-night party: we always called him to give him the heads up. He appreciated this and rewarded us by giving us the combination to the locked gate. He asked us to share it with no one.

Now, the park was ours, or so we felt. No longer did we have to worry about people or dogs interrupting our pups' play. And no longer did we have to clean up for anyone but ourselves. Pinto could hunt gophers, Matty could sniff around for food, and Ringo could meander through the grass, enjoying the sun on his old bones.

CHAPTER THIRTY-ONE

Solo Makes Her Transition.

The lives of our contented little family churned on. Ringo continued to slow down with age, and the whole family made accommodations. We began lifting him up and down from the car when he could no longer jump by himself. Matty and Pinto gave him kisses and let him choose which bed he wanted to rest on when in the family room. They waited patiently at the door to let him walk out first to go potty. He no longer went upstairs, so we made sure he was included in plenty of family time downstairs. And, of course, lots of TV time with dad.

Solo stayed upstairs much of the time now. She and Tinker hung out in our bedroom, only coming down occasionally, not daily like they used to. Solo was declining. She had lost quite a bit of weight and was eating less, but she seemed to be holding her own. She still purred a lot, enjoyed being petted, and loved to snuggle at night.

One day, all of that changed in an instant. I was making the bed in the morning when I noticed Solo laying on the mat in front of the bathroom sink. She was panting vigorously, and it seemed that she couldn't stand up. She was clearly in trouble. I called to George, picked her up, and we rushed her to the animal hospital.

We checked in and sat patiently until the vet came in to examine her. After blood work and a urinalysis, we got the news that she was in acute kidney failure. Her kidneys were no longer filtering her blood and her organs were shutting down. There was nothing to do but help our sweet Solo make her transition.

There are times when the world comes crashing in and nothing seems right. This is one of those times. We love, we nurture, and we play with our beloved fur kids. We know that their lives are short. We prepare ourselves for the day they will leave their physical body behind, but we're never really prepared. It is always a shock when someone tells us, "It's time." It was that time for Solo. George and I stroked her, held her, spoke sweetly to her, told her how deeply she was loved and what a wonderful matriarch she had been to our family. The doctor injected her with the drug that would allow her to drop peacefully into her very last sleep, and we let her go. With very heavy hearts and many tears, we let her go.

CHAPTER THIRTY-TWO

Missing Our Sweet Solo.

A few weeks after making her transition, I got the strong sense that I wanted to connect with Solo in spirit. I missed her so much. George and I also wanted to check in with Tinker and know how she was handling the loss of her sister. Animals often appear to be doing well but there is a posture of stoicism they assume that can be misleading. We wanted to know if Tinker's little heart was okay. And so, of course, we called Amanda.

Amanda: *"When I'm communicating with an animal that's in spirit, it's different for me because I feel like the animal is seeing things from an aerial view. They're not in the moment like our living animals are. It sounds cliché to say they see things like a guardian angel, but that's how it feels to me. I get the big picture instead of the small details. Additionally, when an animal is in spirit, they seem to have a much better view of the future than an animal that is still in physical form. Animal communication never surprises me more than when I'm communicating with an animal in spirit."*

"What would you like to ask Solo?" Amanda asked us.

"What was it like to transition out of her physical body and into spirit? I want to know how she's doing," I said.

"And can she tell us about how to care for Tinker?" George added.

Amanda responded with what she learned from Solo, *"For her, transitioning wasn't this monumental force of energy. It was as simple as the sunrise. It was just a breath of air."*

"The act of removing myself from my body, it was just a breath of fresh air. It was that simple. It was easy, natural. It had such a flow to it. I didn't struggle to rise above my body." Solo told her.

"So, I said, what was the transition like thereafter," Amanda continued. "And I'll be honest with you, Kathy and George, I have asked this question hundreds of times and every time it varies. It's extremely different from animal to animal. As soon as I connected with her, I remembered how intense she was, how large a soul she was. I was expecting her to say something that was really just fireworks in the sky—a big story—and she showed me the sun rising. It just rises. And I said, 'okay, honey, you're making it very simplistic. Can you tell me what it felt like?'"

"I keep showing you the ease of it, the flow of it," Solo continued.

"And she says she really felt like it was the right time to transition and the ease into the flowing of the sun was so perfect because it feels like the weight of the earth was removed. She said that because it's your job, Kathy, it's literally your job to raise the elevation of consciousness as a whole, her (Solo) being on a higher plane, her being up with the sun, being on a higher vibration, makes it so much easier for you to connect to a higher space because of how connected the two of you are," Amanda told me.

"So, let me say this to you differently because I really want you to understand what she means. Because she is on such a high vibration, that, in turn, brings you to a higher space of elevation. Meaning that (my hand is just radiating as I'm communicating with her, she is such an elevated being) let me give you a human example, let me find a good analogy. I'm almost at a loss for words to explain something like this. Let's use scuba diving as an analogy. Let's say that you and George go scuba diving together but you always go tandem, as partners, and he increases his lung capacity somehow by 500% and his ability to handle deeper water and the pressure of the depths so much more so he puts the two of you in some kind of bubble. Now all of a sudden you can go so much deeper because you're with him. That's how what she's showing me feels. It's so hard for me to explain something so great in human words. Because of her elevating, she wants to bring you so much higher. She feels like it is your time, Kathy, to raise everybody's consciousness. For lack of better words, Kathy, I feel like you're going to host this worldwide summit of meditation, and you're going to be the one to facilitate that. I know that sounds really extreme or ridiculous because it sounds so great, but that's how it feels. It feels like you have this really big undertaking, really big path, and Solo is so excited that she's not weighted down to a body, giving you small amounts of help but that she can be in this non-physical form giving you larger amounts of help by helping you to be closer to the sun as she is now.

'There's so much more. Let me wrap my little tiny pea brain around this large presence of hers and give you more. This communication with her is so intense. I'll be honest with you, she's really incredible.

"I have to pause our communication and share something with you. A lot of times when people are calling me and I'm doing a communication with an animal in spirit, it's very simplistic—the animal has been in a physical body and they made a transition to spirit and they miss belly rubs, or treats they used to get and they're going to reincarnate—it's very simplistic. Communicating with her, I feel like I should have first gotten my PhD. She is so intense and so light, and she's taking this communication in a way that is completely unexpected." Amanda stopped a second to catch her breath before she continued.

"She wants to share with me that her timing of passing was very intentional for her. It wasn't that she had been struggling for a while and now she's done struggling. It felt like it was a very purposeful time for her to leave. She said, 'I want to talk to you about what's going on in the world right now.' And I was like, wow, it really took me by surprise for her to say that. She said, 'I want to talk with you about the mass amount of consciousness that's taking place in the world right now.' I asked if she was talking about this crazy virus everyone is freaking out about, but she said it's not just that, there's so much more. The whole purpose of this communication is for her to help us understand what a great leader she is (and when she says leader she means illuminating, like leading people to the Light). I asked her to simplify everything she was showing me. (She is such a high being. I feel like I'm trying to communicate with such a high Goddess that I'm having a hard time understanding the depth of what she's showing me.)

"So, here goes: She says she wants to first start by talking about the fact that the whole world, right now, is in a state of trying to—almost like a mixing of oil and water—there's a lot of separation going on. I asked if she meant religious separation or separation of races."

"No, no, not that type of separation. It's not a separation like segregation that is going to be taking place. It's a separation of those who are ready to evolve and become one with higher consciousness and those who are really struggling to be in the humanness of their human experience, what we would call the rat race. It's really a time that people are separating not so that they can separate but so that they can blossom. That's what's taking place now and my mom understands that on a deeper level," Solo explained.

"My mom is not caught in the mass hysteria of things," Solo continued. "Mom understands that now is the time for people to come together and to raise their vibration. And I mean that in the purest way. When I say raise their vibration, I mean become one. It's almost like a sort of a chanting or a praying that is intentionally raising the vibration. And because of that, it's really important that there are leaders of the Light and there are those that are helping others to understand that now isn't the time to get into political craziness. Let's not start worrying. Let's not panic. That isn't the space. Rather than seeing this time as a disaster or a tragedy, let's look at it as a cleansing of the palate."

Amanda continued, "Honey, you're so far advanced. You're really ahead of me. Bring it down a little bit and help me understand."

"What you need to understand, as a human, is this: your humanness, as a whole, is really not serving you. You're so caught up in the humanness of being human that you're missing the connection to other species: the earth and the animals."

"Yes, I agree with you on all of this. Yes, absolutely," Amanda said.

"No, you're not quite getting it. You're seeing it on a much more selfish level. This isn't just about everyone evolving so that we can have animal liberation. That's coming from a self-serving place and it's not about that. It's about each individual finding what, for them, is their higher self through this," Solo told her.

"Gosh, this is so complicated for me to understand," Amanda replied. "But my takeaway is that when this whole pandemic disaster is over, it would bring insight for personal changes. As an example, I spent a lot more time with my son. For some people, they're stuck with their spouse. They're leaving their relationship, and finding they can be really happy alone. For other people, it could be about spending more time in nature. Maybe for others, it's about foster dogs finding homes, some finding the happiness in the simplicity of just being. Whatever it is, there's not one answer. It's about each individual connecting to what makes them more whole and happier and connects them to the authenticity of their soul and not their humanness like, let's go online, let's go shopping. It's not about everyone finding God. It's not about everyone finding their higher self. It's not about everyone respecting nature or deciding that animals shouldn't be eaten or tortured. It's about each individual finding something that is lighting a small light inside of them so that the world is a little bit more illuminated."

(Amanda got emotional here. "I'm going to start crying," she said.)

Then Amanda said to Solo, "Okay, honey, why are you sharing this with me and, I guess, to be frank, what does this have to do with your mom?"

"It has everything to do with my mom. My mom can really understand this in a way that you can't. I'm kind of stumbling here, but my mom can also understand that it's her job to help each person, in any little way that she can, to become a better version of who they are, and sometimes it's just by being."

"Wow," Amanda responded. "That's really intense and you're right. (Amanda broke up again, "Excuse me, I'm so emotional." She is really incredible.)

She continued. "I said, so how do I translate that, and what do you want me to say?"

"I just want my mom to know that I'm on her side and that I am this ray of sunshine and that I'm with her always," Solo said. "And my job, right now, for her, isn't to rush and to come back and get a new body. My job is to help her raise the level of consciousness. My mom's way of doing that is very gentle. It's the simple act of just being like sometimes when a counselor sits in a room and they're just there holding space for you. Or sometimes it's just bearing witness to someone who is going through a tough time."

"It's just your presence alone, Kathy, that is helping raise the awareness and raise the consciousness and it's not a small job," Amanda told me. "It's a huge job and by Solo being with you, it is raising your vibration, Kathy, which, in turn, helps others to raise their vibration a little higher. It's like if everyone is holding a balloon and you're in a hot air balloon and you're all holding hands. You rise, and then all of a sudden, everyone is going up higher. That's how it feels to me.

"When there is an animal at a very high vibration or a very old soul, a wise soul, we become more intuitive because we're connected to them. When my dog, Tyson, died, I felt like my intuition went from warm to scalding hot. I was seeing and feeling everything. It took me a few weeks to adapt to that because it was my natural response to want to block it out because it was scary. What I feel for you, Kathy, with her passing, is a raised consciousness and a raised vibration and a raised spiritual space. She shows me herself as the sun, I mean literally, I see her as rising with the sun."

"Does she have any tips for me about how to better connect with her?" I asked.

"This is so much easier for me to answer because, wow, when she was talking about the humanness and the mass hysteria of the world, I felt like my head was going to explode as she was showing me all this. I can't see this bigger picture from her perspective because I'm not that wise. Thankfully, when I asked her this, she gave me such a grounded answer. I said, 'Sweetie, tell me everything, how can your mom connect with you and is there anything you want to share with her that's more concrete and less airy?'"

"Yes I would love to talk about those things, but do you understand that what I just told her is the most important thing? Do you understand that navigating these troubling waters is not the end of my mom's job, it's the beginning? It's really important for her to work from a higher platform. So, whatever it is that my mom is doing, it's wonderful, but it needs to be from a higher, elevated platform. She needs to be talking to or coaching or teaching more people. That's a hard thing to do in this moment. It's not my mom's job to do that in this moment, but that will be a part of her soul purpose, her job, her point of being. In the moment, all that my mom is doing is all she needs to do, but when these troubling times are over and we're moving on to the next phase of this cleansing, this evolving, it's really important that my mom's platform becomes larger. Highlight this, it's really important. It's really important for my mom to be seen, because there's a difference when someone sees you. Of course, when someone talks to my mom on the phone they can feel her energy and it feels wonderful and most people can pick up on how authentic she is, but when they're near her, they can physically feel that energy. The warmth of that needs to be felt in person," Solo explained.

Amanda went on, "I asked her, "sweetheart, how can your mom better connect with you?" And she said, 'How can you breathe, you just do it.' I replied with, 'Honey, that's too simple, give me something more instructional.'"

"Now that my mom knows that I'm waiting, alongside her, to help raise the consciousness, it's just a matter of being. It's just a matter of her saying, can you help me?"

Amanda explained it this way. "Turn on the intention and she's there. Turn on the radio and you hear it play. You don't have to think about how you're tuning in. You just turn it on. You make the effort to hit the on switch. It's the same thing in connecting with her. It's simply about saying, can you help me with this and all of a sudden, it's so corny but it's like these heat lamps come on. It just feels radiating."

Amanda spoke directly to me, "Solo was a big part of your work while she was physically in her body and that was important to her, right? And so, now, it's going to be one hundredfold more important that you invite her in while you're working and that you make a conscious effort not only to do that, but to let others know that she is being invited in. It's important to invite her help consciously."

Amanda turned back to Solo. "How can your mom connect with you on an individual level so she can be one with you, connect to you, or have a communication with you? How can I help your mom facilitate that connection between the two of you?"

"Tell my mom that when she closes her eyes, she doesn't need to ask a question. She should just wait for a sign."

"Wait for a sign?" Amanda asked.

"Yes, tell her to close her eyes and just be. Don't try to do any communication. Just close her eyes and wait for a sign."

"And I said to her, that with all due respect, that's not how we communicate with animals," Amanda told us.

"No, no, listen to me, this is my mom and me. I know what I'm doing. You don't know. Listen to me: close your eyes, just be, wait for a sign. That's it. Then the door will be open."

Amanda attempted to explain to me, "Once the door has opened, it will become tangible, something real, and it's going to be easier. You might hear a sound that didn't belong in the room like a tap on the window or a tiny little knock sound, or feeling something on your body. It would be something that doesn't belong. It could be very subtle. But that will be your tangible sign that you've connected with Solo.

"The first time this happens you'll say, 'I get it, she's really here.' It's just that simple. For her, just being, is what it is. She's not in this mystical, magical place that, you know, some of us want to call heaven or the rainbow bridge. She is just being. She is as being as air, or sunlight. She is just a higher vibration of space, and that's where she is. So, when you try to connect with her, don't try to go to an outside place, because she's not an outside place. She IS. It's just as simple as knowing that she's with you."

Amanda then spoke to me, "It's important that you get beyond your grief. You need to fully accept that she's physically gone. Then when she gives you those signs, you'll embrace her fully in spirit.

"I'm going to say something important, and I don't want you to take this lightly. Your connection with her in spirit is going to be the strongest connection that you'll ever have in your life. Solo is such an enlightened being. It's like all of a sudden you're plugged into a Buddha or Allah or Jesus. She is a version of your higher self. You connecting to her will not be just once in a while or just when you need help with clients or raising the consciousness through meditation or anything like that. It's also going to be the little decisions. Should you eat an avocado with breakfast or half an orange or both? It's little things that you wouldn't even think to ask for advice on that you'll just feel her gentle guidance. Her guidance feels strong and powerful and kind, but it also feels very real. I don't think it's going to happen overnight as much as she paints it to be such a simple picture. I don't think it's going to be something that happens tomorrow. I feel like there's going to be several times where you feel or you hear something that I'm going to call tangible that you start to really get that it's Solo. You'll get that she's really present all the time. That isn't cliché. She IS ever present. And then you'll start hearing, 'that's a good idea', 'that's a bad idea', 'do it this way instead.' And then, soon, it's just flowing in. It's just like a thought. You recognize her voice from your own thought but it's five to six times a day, sometimes ten times a day. She is always there to lend a helping hand. Don't expect it tomorrow. Expect it for sure in the next few months. You don't have to remind yourself that she's there. She'll remind you.

"Solo is going to come in when you just close your eyes and you're like, okay, I would really love to feel you. If you're here, I'd love to connect to you. She can navigate around any energy. She's going to come in when you're in that free space, not intensely thinking of her and putting a lot of baggage down. She'll connect with you when you make it easy."

Amanda asked our question for Solo: "Where do you want your physical ashes to be placed?"

"When I connected with her this time, before I could even get this question out, I smelled this something and I don't know exactly how to describe it. It was a very sweet smell, sort of a whipped cream or a vanilla milkshake or some kind of sweet caramel latte. A very sweet smell in the air and it smelled so good. Maybe like a toasted marshmallow. Something that smells very vanilla-y, soft, sweet. It doesn't smell like anything that's in your home and it doesn't smell like you, Kathy. That smell is what she smells like right now. And I asked her, 'Is that what you smell like now?' and she said, 'Yes, so when you smell that smell, it's me.' Oh, my gosh, it gave me goosebumps. 'That makes me really happy. So, your mom is going to smell that smell?'"

"Yes, do you smell it?"

"I smelled it again. It was like someone blending a whipped cream smell. It is a very soft, whipped, vanilla, sweet smell. I can't say that enough. That's her smell. I asked, 'Do you want me to share that with your family?' and she told me that I should."

Then Amanda asked Solo again what she wanted done with her ashes.

"Solo said there's nothing she wants you to do right now. She said just leave them be. I asked if she would like them placed on a mantle, in a meditation space, somewhere special. She said she doesn't want you to place them anywhere where it's going to catch your eye during intimate moments. Not just between you and George, not just sex, but any moments of intimacy. Not near your meditation space. That's an intimate moment, you're connecting with your higher self, with your guides. She doesn't want you to place her ashes near George's spot on the couch because there are intimate moments for him there. She doesn't want them placed near your bedroom. She said she wants them to be placed somewhere like this: she showed me near a window near a dining area because a lot of emotion doesn't go into that space. So, the places in your home that are heavily saturated with energy, she doesn't want to be in those places.

"She's not asking for anything specific. Don't spread them anywhere. Just keep them. When the time is right, she'll guide you to do something different with them. She has no attachment or non-attachment to them. There will be a time in the not-too-distant future where you, Kathy, will be in that easy space and you'll hear her very clearly giving you instructions."

Our time with Amanda was almost up for the day, and we wanted to move our attention to Tinker.

The first question we had for Tinker was, "Let her know what happened with Solo, and ask her what we can do to help her feel better. She seems anxious. She has never been clingy but she is now. She wants to be close more so than ever. We think she may be feeling alone or vulnerable."

Amanda replied, "When I tried to connect to Tinker, Solo was like, 'Wait a second, you're not going anywhere, we weren't finished.' And I said, 'I'm so sorry, forgive me. What aren't you finished with? What do you want to say?'"

Solo said, "I want to tell my dad how much I appreciate all that he did for me and how much he really opened up. I give myself a lot of credit for that. My dad is really a dog person through and through, but I really felt like he opened up to me so much and he opened up because of me, and I feel like he taught me as much as I taught him."

"Wow, would you like to share that with me?" Amanda asked.

"No, he knows what I mean," Solo responded.

"She feels like you taught each other about breaking down walls," Amanda expressed to George.

And then Solo said to Amanda: "I didn't have a chance to tell my mom..." (Amanda said, "I'm sorry, I'm going to cry.") "...I want to tell my mom how much I infinitely love her, how much she means to me, how much she always meant to me, how much she loved me with so much depth and passion, how much she's my person, how much she's my soul sister, my soul sister, my soul sister, I can't say that word enough times, how much I love her, how many lifetimes I've loved her for, how many lifetimes we've shared together. We've been best friends, we've been twins, we've been sisters, we've been everything. She is my person. If there's ever a lifetime where I'm on a physical plane and I'm a physical being, I'll always choose to walk that path with her. We'll always reincarnate together. I'll always come back in physical form near her. If there is ever a lifetime where I'm living on the earth plane, I will always be a physical being near her. I can't help it. I can't be any other way. She is my best friend. I love her so, so much. She always has a way of making me feel so special and she makes me radiate."

"Okay, anything else?" Amanda asked.

And Solo said, "Everything else. I love her so much. I need her to hear the words love, love, love, because I love her so much. And tell her thank you so much for being with me and for being so gentle with me. Tell her thank you for putting up with me when I was young and a tomboy. I always got nothing but acceptance. Can you tell her I'm strong again? I've missed being strong. That was the one hard part about my passing, the time leading up to it when I wasn't strong any longer and I wasn't myself. But I have regained all of my strength."

"It wasn't just the physical strength that was a hard loss," Solo continued. "It was maintaining that I was still mentally and physically strong when I felt like there were times when I wasn't, but my mom held the weight for both of us. She never looked at me like I was less than. Never looked at me like I was weak or feeble. Helping me remain with such dignity was so important and it was more valuable than words could possibly begin to describe. Just tell her how much I love her and tell her that I will always be with her. Tell her that she'll see me again and she'll feel me again and she'll know me again and that this is really the beginning of our next chapter of being sisters all over again and in a much more powerful, much more substantial way. There is substance, there is so much substance to what lies before us."

"I'll tell her all those things. Are you done now?" Amanda asked.

"For now. You'll probably be hearing from me soon," Solo finished.

"So, when an animal has said that to me before, I will literally email someone at 3 o'clock in the morning because I'm repeatedly having a knock on the door. This happens when an animal is trying to get a message through to their person and they're not hearing. So, if that happens, forgive me. If I'm disturbed, you're disturbed, that's my rule," Amanda said.

Back to Tinker: Amanda asked, "Do you want to show me how you're doing with your sister's passing?"

And Tinker replied, "For me, the hardest part isn't the loss of her. The hardest part is trying to be okay and figure out what my role is without having someone to be the leader. I don't know how to be strong on my own."

(At this point Amanda left to let her cat in who was suddenly fiercely meowing at the door. She told us that this cat always comes to hold space whenever there is an animal in need. It appeared that he was coming to hold space for Tinker.)

"For Tinker, being the brave one, being the strong one, being the big sister, that's not her strong suit. She understands that Solo is gone, that she left her physical body. She also understood that the entire time that Solo was struggling, going through some physical challenges, she understood that it was her body telling her, time is almost up, time is almost up. And she'd be like, oh, but you can't leave me because I'm not ready for this role on my own. I'm not prepared. It's like all of a sudden the older sister turning the car keys over to the younger sister and saying, 'Okay, you've got to do it all on your own now.' It's scary. And that's the scary part for her. The anxiety is not because she doesn't know where her sister is. The anxiety is not even caused by missing her because she doesn't see her as gone. She is very present. No, Tinker faces this reality—holy shit, I've got to do this on my own. This is scary. She wants to hide behind Solo, but Solo's not there physically to hide behind. That's the scary part. That's the anxiety that you're describing."

Amanda asked Tinker, "What can we do to make you more comfortable and ease you into this new role of being on your own?"

Amanda explained, "She really saw Solo as having the role of the big sister. A human example: you jump in the water first and make sure it's not too hot or too cold. You taste the food first and make sure it's not spoiled. That's how it feels. Now all of a sudden, Tinker is scared.

"She showed me the feeling of how it's scary, overwhelming. I said, 'Sweetie, I understand, you've shown me the feeling probably five or six times, but you're not giving me a solution.'"

"That's all I know. Do you understand that I'm not as wise as her?" Tinker asked Amanda. "Do you understand that I'm not as old as her?"

"As in physical years?" Amanda asked.

"No, in energy years."

"She sees herself as maybe being 50 years old in total years in lifetimes, whereas she sees Solo as being 2000 years old. They weren't comparable energetically. When I'm asking her how do we make you feel better, less anxious, she just keeps repeating the emotions over and over to me," Amanda told us.

"How about if I make some suggestions. How about if they give you some different type of treats or some new toys?" Amanda asked her. "I feel if looks could kill, I would have gotten every dirty look. 'That was such a stupid response. That was so basic,' Tinker said. So, I asked, 'What will make you feel better?' I feel like she has to grow into the role on her own and there's nothing that can help that. It's just time and age. She feels so young because she has had this protective energy of her sister around her all the time, making her more confident, and without that, she is less confident. There comes the anxiety. With a little bit of time, it should help bring her out of her shell."

Amanda continued, "So, that seems like such a bland answer, but that's really the answer. There is nothing you can say or do that can help her heal any wound because she's not feeling that. She's feeling the anxiety of being alone. For Tinker, living in her own light, without Solo, is a new experience. With a little time you'll notice her confidence is going to build. The worst thing you can do is to pressure her into being with the rest of the family. Just give her time. Give her space."

To close, Amanda told us the story of Garfield, the foster cat that her son insisted on getting. He's the cat who now holds space for Amanda's animal clients who are in need. He came to hold space for Tinker.

CHAPTER THIRTY-THREE

Tinker Becomes Brave.

There is no way to deny how much we all missed Solo. Her very presence made everyone feel seen and welcome, family and friends alike. Even my social media family missed her. Each Thursday night, when I logged on to Facebook to lead group chanting, Solo always came along to assist. She would sit on my lap, look into the camera, sashay and purr, all small acts of connection. When I hosted wisdom circles or kirtans at my home, Solo greeted our guests, making sure each person felt included. Everyone loved Solo.

But life keeps flowing and we find that we get caught up in the current of living our lives, even as we are grieving our losses. This is how our spirit begins to heal. We find ways to move forward. We teach ourselves how to embrace the simple acts of breathing, of eating, of being in community without the physical presence of our beloved.

Tinker was amongst those of us who learned how to navigate within this new paradigm of a home without Solo. Little by little, she began to venture down the stairs, to sit with us in the family room. She enjoyed starting her day on the back of the couch, looking out the living room windows at neighbors as they walked their dogs or clocked their morning run. She was becoming brave as she asserted herself to claim a favorite place on the arm of a chair or the warm lap of her humans. She seemed to enjoy hanging out with her canine brothers. Ringo, Matty, and Pinto each invited her into their circle with a gentleness that was precious to witness.

The energy in our home clearly shifted when Solo left her body. And, as Solo had predicted, Ringo was moving closer to the time that he, too, would make his transition. He was spending much more time sleeping deeply. At times his breath would become so shallow that it was almost imperceptible. I found myself creeping up to him as quietly as I could, to make sure he was still breathing, to make sure he was still alive. His mobility worsened and he always needed assistance getting up. He was becoming incontinent, having accidents in the house. At times, he seemed like he had faded mentally as he ambled toward a corner of the room and simply stood there until we called him away. His hearing and his vision had faded. Our big, beautiful boy was slipping away. I wondered, each night, if we would wake up in the morning and find that he had left his body.

It was time to talk to Ringo to learn what his wishes were.

Baby Ringo and Big Sister Westy

George & Kathy Hiking

Kathy with Pinto, Matty & Ringo

Kathy writing Nina sleeping

Baby Ringo

George with Nina & Abbie

Nina & Abbie as babies

Me & the bcs

Abbie & Nina

Nina kissing Kathy

CHAPTER THIRTY-FOUR
Ringo Tells Us: I Only Want to Die Once.

Amanda liked to give an animal the floor to say whatever they want to say before we humans begin to ask questions or tell them things. She did this with Ringo and here is the first thing that he said:

"I need for my parents to understand that I only want to die one time, one day, for one minute, and that's it. I don't want to die a million times in their minds prior to that one time. That's what's happening now."

Amanda said, "Yes, I understand. What can I explain to them about your journey?"

"My journey is infinite. You understand this is only a stepping stone? Do you understand that when I come back I'm just going to be like this?"

"He showed me that he's going to come out of the water and be new again," Amanda told us. "And I asked him, come out of the water, what does that mean?"

"Well, changing. I'm just describing it to you figuratively. You shouldn't read too much into that. Just listen to what I'm saying and stop trying to analyze everything."

"Ringo told me that it's really annoying. I said, 'I'm sorry, I'm so sorry.'"

"Just listen to what I'm saying," Ringo told her. "I'm 13 and I've had a really long life. I've had a lot of great journeys and I've had a lot of enjoyment. I've had a lot of love. I've had a lot of moments of serenity and peace and there's a lot of laughter, a lot of understanding, a lot of patience, a lot of love. My parents understand all this more than anyone. The journey of my soul is infinite. When I leave my physical body, it is important for me that when I leave they understand they are not saying goodbye. Don't say the word goodbye. It is so ugly. I'll see you in a little bit, I'll see you in a little bit, I'll see you in a little bit. That's what I want them to say to me."

"Honey, do you want to go naturally on your own or do you want assistance?" Amanda asked him. "And he said, 'No, no, I don't want to go naturally.' I asked, how come? And he said because he doesn't like the idea of things dragging out. He said he also feels like it will be much easier because you keep mentally thinking about his death."

Amanda told us, "I'm sure you don't want to, but mentally you're taking yourself to that place. When you're taking yourself to that place, he's going with you. He feels the energy of that. It's like you're turning on the radio and even if you don't plan on listening to it, it doesn't matter because anyone with ears could hear it as well. And so, he's replaying that with you. He says he wants to go there, to die, only one time, so he also feels like it would be easier for you if you set a date and you mark it on the calendar and you know that on this specific day of this specific month, that's the day that he's going to leave. You know you have to deal with it on that day, but you will also understand you don't have to deal with it until that day comes."

"If we do it that way," Ringo said, "my mom and dad won't have such a hard time with it. They need to know that it's very temporary and that when I leave, I'm coming right back to enjoy the simplicity of life again. I have a hard time thinking about coming back and being a dog. Part of me would rather be a cat. Because if I'm a cat, I get to do what I love to do."

"I asked, what's that," Amanda said. "And he said, a whole lot of nothing. He said he's at the point in his life where he really enjoys just being. Sitting around. Just lounging. Listening to noises. Listening to talking. He enjoys listening when you guys are talking. He enjoys listening to that sound. He very much enjoys watching television, just lying in front of the couch and doing nothing. And he likes the idea of continuing that.

"He said if he comes back and he is a dog again he would have to go through the entire stage of being a puppy. He would have to feel like he has to go do things, go on nature hikes, go places. He just doesn't really want that. He says he loves the simplicity of life the way it is right now. So, he would like to continue having the simplicity of that and he feels like by being a cat he could just do that all the time. He could just lounge. Humans don't have such high expectations for you. Maybe it's socialization, maybe it's interacting with other dogs. It feels like the bar is much higher for a puppy than if he were to choose to come in and be a cat."

Ringo said, "Do you understand that if I'm a cat I could just lay around and watch TV. I could be a couch potato. I could just lounge and play when I feel like it and for the rest of the time, very low expectation."

Ringo continued, "Another thing that's really important to me is that so many times I wish I could be little so that I could do things that I can't do because of my size. You know I'm 50 pounds, right? If I was little, I could jump on things, jump on people. I would love to do that. If I'm a cat, I would have the freedom to do that."

"He pictures himself just coming over and sitting on your lap, just hanging out with you and doing nothing. Being able to share that closeness and that bond is something he can't do now because he's so big. 'I'm not huge, but I'm not a cat,' he said."

"I have enjoyed the journey of being a dog so much, and I had a lot of fun dog adventures, but I want to experience something new. I want to have a different journey, but the same journey."

Amanda asked him to explain that. "What do you mean?"

He replied, "A different journey, experiencing things from a different size, but the same journey, being back with my soul family. That's where I belong. They are where I belong. Their home is a place of love and peace and acceptance and I love being there.

"I would have no choice but to come back whether I come back as a cat or whether I come back as a dog or whether I just stay there as a spirit. But I don't want to be a spirit. I love being in a physical body. No matter what, no matter who I am, I'm coming home."

Ringo asked Amanda, "Do they understand that on the day of my death that it is just a stepping stone to come right back home again?"

She replied, "Yes, I'll explain that to them very thoroughly."

"But can you tell them a thing that's really important?" he asked.

"What is important?"

"I love the way I look. I absolutely love the way that I look. I think I'm extraordinarily handsome. I think that I'm so so so so so so good looking and whether I come back as a dog again, or whether I come back as a cat, I'm going to look exactly the same. I'm going to have the same markings. I'm going to be the same colors and I'm going to have these same striking eyes that when you look at me you'll say, ahh they're such soulful eyes."

"I got it," Amanda told him. "That makes me feel so much better than what you said before."

"That's because you were trying to interpret what I said before," Ringo continued. "If you were just listening to me and you weren't trying to understand it, you would have seen how easy it is.

"My family is predicting, my mom especially, is predicting my death. She's so worried about it that she is thinking about it on a regular basis and so she is playing it like a bullhorn for me to hear. She sneaks up and stands beside me to monitor my breath. She thinks I don't know, but I do, and it upsets me. I don't want to think about it. I want to deal with it once and that's it. It wasn't that complicated. You made something very simple very complicated by overthinking it."

"I'm so sorry," Amanda said

"That's okay, my family needs to hear these simple things. Don't make them complicated."

"Okay, I got it," she reassured him.

Amanda addressed George and me. "I'm sorry I'm talking so fast, there was so much that I wanted to relay before I started forgetting. So tell me what you think, what you want to say or what you want to ask?"

"I want to know if he is in pain. Are there any things that we can do right now to make his life better?" George asked.

"Those are great questions, but before we switch gears and take it to the physical, he is very much in tune right now with his spiritual. So, before we switch gears, for myself as well as for him, is there any clarification or any questions that you guys have in regards to his spiritual journey now or thereafter?"

I said to Amanda, "For me, what you just told me about what he said has given me a lot more clarity and a lot more peace and he's absolutely right, I've been, well, I watch his breathing, I look at him all the time to see if he's still with us and I don't want him to be in pain and so, I have the question floating around my head, should we help him to transition and if so, when should we do that. And so he's right, I've been going through that all the time, every day.

"I want you to tell him that I acknowledge that I've been doing that and I'm going to really work on changing that pattern and just try to enjoy every moment that he's here. I also want him to know that I completely understand and embrace his infinite being and that, for me, if he comes back to us in spirit, I would love that. If he comes back to us as a kitty that's white and black with beautiful, soulful eyes, I will embrace that, and if he comes back as another puppy, I will embrace that. Any way that he wants to come home."

"I will relay all of this to him, and I will ask him the question. I will be really honest with you, I feel like, for him, the biggest thing that he wants to talk about is his journey and his excitement around this, what's next. More so than the physical because he is very close to passing. When an animal gets very close to passing, although their physical bodies are still operating, they are on an elevated level. It's almost like when someone has an adrenaline rush. When an animal is very close to crossing over, their physical body is alive and it may look like it's struggling or suffering, but they're on this kind of adrenalin rush, so to speak. They're not feeling as much as we think they're experiencing because they're moving on to the next journey and they're getting excited about what's next and they're feeling that high vibration of the afterlife. And so, I will of course ask him all of those physical questions but, for me, it feels like when I give him the reins to take the communication where he sees fit, he really wants to talk about his one moment of death and his journey thereafter. He doesn't want to talk so much about what he is physically experiencing in the moment because to him that's very unimportant. It's very small in comparison to the big picture of his rebirth. I will ask him those questions, George. Give me a few minutes and I'm going to open the door for him."

Amanda left the phone for about three minutes to ask Ringo our questions about his physical well-being.

"So, let me start with the physical stuff: He said it is an absolute, absolute, absolute that for him the lack of mobility, the feeling like he is (I don't like this word, but this is the word he uses) crippled. I said, 'That's such a horrible word' and he said, 'But that's what it is.' He said he feels like his body is just crippled. The idea of getting up or walking is absolutely the most unappealing thing. He wants to share with you that it isn't just right now that he is out of sorts and that he's not in his right state of mind but this has been going on for a long time, like months, maybe 10 months or close to a year that he has what he describes as sundowners or dementia where he is just not in his mind. Literally, his mind is one place, but his spirit and soul are in a separate space. They are not one and the same," Amanda said.

"My mind has been wandering for a long time. The best human word I know to describe it would be sundowners but I'm not just getting it at sundown. It's something I have consistently. Like my mind is just spacey. That's not a bad thing because when I'm going to this other place and I'm not in my right mind, it's a good place. It's not a place of my body suffering," Ringo told her.

"It's like he's doing himself a great service by taking his mind away from the now and the present struggles of his physical body. So, this dementia that he has created for himself is a way out of experiencing the physical pain. For him, it's very simple. It's not a bad thing. Is he in pain? No, he's really not. He's so much further than that. He's out of his mind so often, but his body is declining and this has been a very long process of decline," Amanda shared.

"This has been a very long, long journey of walking downhill," Ringo told her. "I want to be very clear that I'm ready when they're ready. I was actually ready a few months ago. But I'm staying here because I know how much I'm loved and I love it here so much. Also, I didn't want to leave at the same time my sister, Solo, was leaving her body. That would have been too much for my mom and dad. But, it's getting very close to what could be my due date."

"What do you mean?" Amanda asked him.

"My next incarnation. I'm ready to go at any time. When I pass, I want them to not hang on to any physical constraints of my body."

"What do you mean by that. Can you explain?" she asked.

"No, just say it as it is. If they need clarification, I'll give it to them, but please stop trying to analyze me."

She told him, "I'm so sorry I'm doing that."

"That's okay, but overthinking is a problem."

Amanda continued, "I understand. But, honey, do you understand that I'm just trying to help you?"

"Of course I do, but the message is for my mom and my dad, not for you to decipher for them."

Amanda told us, "He wants to let you know that when he passes he wants you to release and allow, release and allow. He repeats that three times, release and allow. Release my body and allow me to come back. But if, when he dies, you're still holding on to that attachment of him and his physical form, and how great he was when he was alive, you're not going to free yourself up for allowing him to come back. When he dies, that's his death. It's that one minute of death. Be done with him. Let his old body go so that his new body can come in. He's really, really adamant about that. So don't hold on to his physical attachment. Not many animals tell me that but he's very, very, very adamant about it. Don't get an urn, lock it, look at it all the time. Just let it go, that's not him. Just the way that you wouldn't hold on to an old shoe, don't hold on to his body because it's not serving him. I'm not saying to just dispose of his body. If you want to have them cremate him and you want to hold on to those ashes, fine, but out of sight, out of mind until that new form comes back because he doesn't want you holding on to the attachment of his old form. That's reliving it and as he says, he only wants his death to happen once."

Amanda returned to her conversation with Ringo, "I asked him if he can tell me about anything he wants to mention or talk about physically. He said, 'I want to talk about the fact that there is nothing to talk about.'"

"He's on a really high playing field. He's on a very high, very elevated spiritual state because he's so excited about his rebirth. He's so excited about taking you guys through the process of him coming back. And if he comes back as a cat, he's thinking like, this is so weird because you'll say, this is a cat, but this cat is exactly like a dog. That in itself is uncommon but it's even more uncommon that your cat is going to be exactly like a dog that was a Border Collie. You'll say, this is just weird but they are so identical. And because he wants to take you through that process of how infinite life is and how unlimited possibilities are, he wants to come back as a cat way more than a dog. I asked him to explain to me why. He said that when he was young he did a lot of fun things, and you (mom and dad) were at a point in your lives that you were active and so, you did lots of things with him. You went places with him. He was a sportsman, and he did a lot of chasing, and a lot of running, and a lot of agility, and a lot of showing off his abilities. He's now at the point where competition doesn't matter to him. He feels like he has evolved from that. So, for him the idea of coming back and having those same earthly possessions feels very petty to him. He feels like where he's at in his evolution, with age he has evolved into realizing what really matters and being competitive doesn't. But if he comes back as a dog, he will have no choice because those things are just innately in you," she explained.

"No, that's not true," Amanda said to him. "There are a lot of dogs that are just lazy dogs and they don't want to do a lot even from puppyhood."

Ringo answered, "But that wouldn't be me because I'm me. I would come back and I would have those same desires and it would take me so long to grow up and I don't want to have to go through that again."

"He feels like in being a cat he could mature much younger," Amanda responded.

"Okay, I respect your thoughts and your feelings," she said. "So, you are definitely leaning towards being a cat?"

"Absolutely I am," he told Amanda. "And explain that to my mom and she will understand why. The prospects of having to do socialization and these active sports, that sounds to me so draining as opposed to just living and being."

"Do you guys understand why he feels this way, Kathy, George?" Amanda asked us.

We both said, "Absolutely."

"So, for him, coming home feels... well, I'm positive that he's coming home within a short period of time. I am borderline wanting to start crying because I am so excited for him because he's so excited. It's almost like he's going to leave, shower and come right back. That's how it feels, like, 'I'm going to hurry and get ready.' It won't be years, but months from the time he passes to the time he comes back. He doesn't have the exact number because he's still in his physical body, but to me it feels like only a few months."

Amanda asked him, "Do you understand that when you're a cat you will have some clear cat DNA. Species have different qualities."

"Yes, I understand that I will be in a different body and do you understand how excited I am to be in a different body because it will be so much more provocative, (he uses this word provocative) to be exactly the same being in a completely different body?"

Amanda answered, "Yes, that's quite a challenge."

"I'm going to show them that. I'm up for the challenge. If someone has a dog and they say, oh that's just like my other dog reincarnated, you'd be like, yeah, not that big a deal, right? Almost kind of like you shrug. But if I have a cat and he is EXACTLY like my Border Collie and it's unbelievable how identical they are, it's amazing. They'll think, I've never met such identical beings let alone two of different species. Then it is extraordinary. I'm ready to do the extraordinary."

"Okay, I got it, I understand," Amanda told him. "So, for him, he's very, very excited about the prospect of not just taking you down the path of reincarnation, because of the beauty of how infinite that feels, but how infinite and blessed it is to go into a different species entirely.

"I feel that I can say with very positive, absolute certainty that not only is he coming back in a very short period of time, but the idea of coming back as a cat is just... oh my gosh, that is such a better idea than being a dog. He says being a dog is too much work. He said, 'I'm really ready for the retirement phase of my life.' He really enjoys not being super active, doing something once in a while but then coming home and just being. He really loves just being in the moment and enjoying the simplicity of life. It feels to me like I'm talking to someone who wants to have a life of retirement. He likes this phase of his life so much, of just being vs. when he was young and doing, doing, doing.

"So, in a nutshell, as a recap going over the most important things that he said thus far: Whenever you choose, he's ready to go. He's already planning the next journey. I hate to say that he is a shell, but it feels like that's a very accurate thing for me to say. So, whenever you're ready, he's ready, but please be sad once, be sad and be done being sad because he's so excited (I literally have goosebumps for him right now) because he is so excited about coming back. He's so excited about jumping up on high things. So excited about being able to come and crawl up and sit on your lap, excited about the ability to have this unlimited mobility. He's very excited about that. So, after he passes, get on board. Get on that same train of excitement in all the details that he's excited about. All those things that he's excited about, get excited with him. He's ready to move along. He's saying, mom and dad, get over it. We're moving along. There's not a lot of sympathy for understanding your point of view (of sadness to let him go)."

At this point, I told her about our Tinker and how she didn't welcome other cats into the house. Tinker would terrorize a new cat. "So, what happens when we meet the new Ringo and we can't bring him home?" I asked her.

"That is a challenge. Let's hear what he has to say about this. I'm sure his answer will be something delightful," Amanda replied.

Amanda left the phone for about three minutes to speak with Ringo about this.

"Wow, wow, wow," she said. "Gosh, he's so amazing. I really like him. I asked him if he wanted to share with me what the issue is moving forward with Tinker and him being rejected by her and I said, 'Honey I understand what great chaos that can cause so let me share with you the issue, the quandary, the problem that lies ahead.'"

"That's ridiculous. I am not a cat coming in," Ringo told her. "They will recognize me with absolute certainty that it is me coming in. I'm not going to be just a cat. A cat is the embodiment of being a cat. They have cat qualities, so they're going to have tension. But I am not just a cat, I am me, taking on the role of a cat for a while. Imagine if my mom dressed up as a man and she put on a mustache and she went shopping at the mall. She does this for one day. She went as a man to see how men get treated. She's not a man, she's just dressing up as one for a little while."

"Do you understand though, how difficult it will be to have this blind faith in just bringing in a kitten, or a young cat, when there are already very established boundaries with the other animals in the home?" Amanda asked him.

"Do you not understand?" Ringo asked.

"I'm so sorry, I don't, and I don't think your parents will either, so, I want to get it right to help them to understand," she replied.

"Please understand that when everybody looks at me, whether it's my parents, whether it's other cats in the home, whether it's the dogs, whether it's strangers, they're going to come over—strangers—and think, oh my god, is that real? He looks so different but he looks exactly the same. This is borderline eerie, that's really weird, your cat is a dog. And your dog is a cat. That's so weird, because it's sooo obvious. Because it's so like, duh, it's me. So, that being said, how would it be a problem? I'm not going to be a cat. I'm going to be myself, being a cat."

"I told him, 'I got it.' For him it's like, duh. That is the word I would use to describe his answer," Amanda said.

"He's very positive about it. And because animals are so much wiser than us, they see the big picture. They have the aerial view so much more than *we humans do. He understands that he would never, ever, ever choose a role that couldn't be fulfilled. He is coming home with a purpose of coming home. He doesn't love being in a physical body so much that he's just choosing to reincarnate to experience the physical world again. His purpose is to stay with his soul family. If he couldn't come back in a physical form, he would have stayed in the spirit world. But he knows he can so that's why he is choosing to come back in a physical body and he is very clearly and very specifically wants the experience of being a cat, to prove to everybody how infinite he is and how infinite transition is and how death is just a one minute process. That's it."*

All I could say was, "Cool!!"

"Cool is right!!" Amanda agreed. "I'm feeling humbled. This has definitely been enlightening for me.

"One more thing... He's going to have a peculiar evolution as a cat. It may not be right away, it may take a year before you see it, but as the months pass, it will become more and more obvious. In the beginning, you're going to see a cat with some of Ringo's personality traits, with the embodiment of Ringo. After you've had him for about two years, you're going to literally forget that he was once a dog and now he's a cat. You're only going to see him as the being underneath. There will not be any differences. Meaning, any of his weird quirks as a cat will make sense because he was a dog. He's going to have something to do with water. He has mentioned water several times. I think he's going to really like water. He's going to like coming into the bathroom when someone is taking a shower or taking a bath. He's going to want to be near water. I don't know that he's going to want to get into the water himself, but you're going to notice that he, as a cat, has an affection for water. It will be something that is absolutely a part of his personality trait. Because he had an affection for water before. He wants to carry something with him from one form to another, and that, for him, is water. He's feeling that this is not a cat quality. If he can bring that quality through as a cat, that would be a confirmation that, look (!!) it's me all over again.

"Remember, he's not coming in again just to be with his soul family. He is coming in with something to prove. He wants to teach us all that life is infinite—death is a one-minute process. We can come in many different forms and many different species and still be the exact same being. He's coming in with this lesson to teach."

With that, our conversation with Amanda ended.

CHAPTER THIRTY-FIVE
Ringo Leaves His Body.

Love Warrior

There is a Divine Pain that is present on the inside of Love.

There is a constant practice required. A practice of letting go of what was in order to learn how to give the love-embrace to what is. It is a practice of learning to love anew in each moment.

How can I love the dead bird on my porch when I know she was the one singing her seductive night song to me during that quiet time just before the sun rose?

How can I love the rose's petals, brown and dry on the ground when just days before I was rejoicing in the beauty of her vibrant color?

How can I love the children who have grown from the babies I held in my arms? Those babes whose sweet milk-breath intoxicated me and caused my mother's heart to swoon with a love so tender. They're gone now, those babies. How can I find a way to let the grief of my loss usher me to a new moment of love?

Real Love, I believe, is a Deep Spiritual Practice. A prayer whispered in each new moment. An intentional opening of the heart to feel the embrace of THIS moment. It takes clear eyes and a strong, curious heart. Real Love is not for the timid. It is a practice for a courageous warrior.

Let me be that warrior.

Kathy Bolte—August 5, 2019

My love for Ringo was, for me, a deep spiritual practice. Loving him so completely required me to become that fully committed love warrior. It was time to help our precious boy make his transition out of body and into spirit. This would require selflessness. It would be one of the hardest things I've ever done. The only thing that allowed me to feel my way through it was my ability to embrace the knowledge that he would come back to us. The plans were laid. It was time to move forward.

It was not long after our conversation with Ringo that it became apparent it was time to make arrangements to help him make his transition. During our last call with Amanda, we learned how important it was for Ringo to "only die once." We also learned how excited he was about shedding his old body and coming back into a new body with an entirely new life.

We became aware of an organization called *Lap of Love*, an organization that employs a host of veterinarians who come to the home to assist pets in making their transition. We called to make an appointment.

Even though we'd been given a thorough "Transition 101" education straight from Ringo, instructing us to avoid grieving over him leaving his physical body. Even though we'd been assured that he would be coming back to us in short order. Even though we were excited about experiencing Ringo as a cat. None of this helped us feel any less heavy with the pain of having to say goodbye to our precious boy.

I believe most humans acknowledge birth as a little miracle. We all get excited over the idea of a human growing in the womb of its mother and then being delivered into the world. A brand new being. A life to celebrate. An adventure to begin. But not many in our Western culture view death as a miracle—one that can rival any birth in its mystery and wonder, and in its infinite promise.

We had learned so many deep lessons from each of our animals. We embraced a clear understanding of the infinite nature of the soul. We understood that the body was just a temporary vehicle for housing the soul. We knew that when the physical body was worn out and needed to be released, the soul would live on, either in spirit or through reincarnation into another physical body.

But how does one release the desire to hold on to what we know? How does one let go of the precious being we have loved so deeply? What will replace that act of burying one's face into the fur of a noble dog who has served us, loved and entertained us. How will we not be haunted by the empty crate, the retired food bowl, his collar and leash? How can we feel our way through gathering the toys that will be left behind, the toys that he claimed as his own? How can we not be visited by the memory of the steady gaze of those intelligent eyes?

Lap of Love was due at our house within the hour. We sat on the floor in the family room, next to Ringo on his bed, Matty, sitting close by, and Pinto curled up on the couch under his blanket. We stroked his head, talked to him and played a little game of "speak", giving him plenty of delicious treats. When we said to speak, he gave us his hushed bark, the one we referred to as his "indoor voice." I had taught him early on to speak quietly when he wanted something, so this little muffled bark was a product of his life of being a gentleman when speaking indoors.

Soon there was a knock on the door. We opened the door to the kind veterinarian who came to help Ringo. She came with the stereotypical "doctor bag" that would hold all she needed to ease Ringo out of his body and release him to spirit.

She began by asking us a number of questions to assess his physical condition. She agreed that the time was right to release him. We asked if Matty and Pinto could stay in the room so that they would understand what was happening and she agreed that it would be a good idea. She also gave us permission to stay with him as long as we wanted before she began the task of giving him that injection that would ease him into a deep sleep. We told her that we were prepared, and that we were ready.

She spoke to him kindly as she gave him the first injection to relax him. Within minutes we could see his muscles ease into a state of relaxation. Then, with a nod to us that said, *Okay, this is it,* she gave him the second injection that causes the heart to stop beating within about three minutes. Though Ringo's musculoskeletal system was a mess, his cardiovascular system was still strong. It took far longer than the usual three minutes for his heart to stop. Our amazing boy remained strong and vital until the very end.

Once his heart had stopped beating, the doctor took some time with her stethoscope, listening for any sign of life. After what seemed like an eternity, she said to us, "He's gone." Those two simple words released the river of tears that had been building up in our hearts. Today was the day we had to let go of our sweet boy. The vet excused herself, said she would give us some time alone with his body. This is when Matty and Pinto got to come near and sniff Ringo's body with all the love and tenderness they showed him throughout their lives together. We wept. We touched him, stroked him, kissed him for the last time. This was the beginning of a time of deep grief and mourning for all of us.

The doctor came back into the house with a stretcher appropriate for a dog of Ringo's size. The three of us lifted his body onto the stretcher. The doctor covered his body with a blanket that looked so comfy. I'm sure he would have loved it. And then we carried him out to her car. And they were gone.

We wept bitter tears of longing and letting go. We took a couple of days off work so we could gather close and support one another and our pups through those first days of missing our boy. It would be about two weeks before his ashes were returned to us. Upon receiving the sacred package, accompanied by that tear-jerker Rainbow

Bridge poem, we wept again. Then we put the box containing his ashes up on the bookshelf and began dreaming of a new kitten coming to live with us.

After about a month we had eased ourselves back into the rhythm of routine. We decided we needed some direction about how and when to find this Ringo kitten.

We called Amanda.

CHAPTER THIRTY-SIX

What? Another Border Collie?

By now, we had come to love Amanda for all that she is and all the gifts she had given us. We chatted a bit, about life and loss. And we told her we felt it was time to speak to Ringo in spirit.

"It's so interesting that you say this because last night I had this really strange dream about a dog who is in spirit and I couldn't see who the dog was. He was telling me, clearly, 'I think I just want to go be with a new family. I want to have adventures. I want to have fun. I want to swim in the rivers. I want to wake up with children screaming every day. I want to eat some of their pancakes under the table.' He was like describing all of these adventurous things and I was like, Okay, why are you telling me this and who, even are you. I was asleep, so, I wasn't even really dissecting it much. I'm really wondering if that was him transmuting that information in my sleep." Amanda shared her dream with us.

We asked her to start by asking Ringo what he had to say about all of this.

She spoke with Ringo and reported this to us:

"He's so intense. I asked him, 'Can you tell me a little bit about what you're doing.'"

He said, "You're finally listening to me? I have been waiting to talk to you for so long and you're finally listening to me. You're finally making time for me?"

Amanda said, "I'm so sorry you've been waiting." She shared the exchange between them.

"I've been waiting and I've been poking you, and I've been prodding you and I've been tapping you on your temples." Ringo said.

"I'm so sorry, honey. I'm oblivious because I tune out and I'm so sorry. What is it that you want to talk to me about?"

"Well, first, I want you to understand that I'm disgruntled that you took so long to listen to me."

"Okay, I acknowledge that," Amanda agreed.

"It's okay, we can move on now, I'm over it."

"So, tell me a little bit about what's going on with you," she asked.

"I'm really, really eager to get into a body. I really want this to happen, and I want it to happen before the summer."

"In the next 5 to 6 months?" Amanda asked him.

"Yeah, I thought it was going to be already, but there are just so many changes happening in the world."

"Yes, there are," Amanda agreed again.

And he said, "There are a lot of thoughts of maybe reconsidering."

"For you or for your family?" she asked.

"For all of us. I thought it over in great detail, over and over. I dissected the idea many times and I just don't want to come back as a cat. I would be so bored. I wouldn't be able to handle it. I want to go outside and smell the fresh air. I love the smell of the salt in the air. And I love the mossy oak smell. And I love the smell of algae in the air as well."

"Like a lot of earthy smells?" she asked him.

Ringo had a lot to tell her. "Yes, earth and water combined. I love that. I want to be part of that. I love my family immensely. I love them more than anything, and I know when the time is right we'll all be together again, but it's not negotiable for me to not come back as a dog who has these adventures. I need to have these adventures. So, I'm really going to turn it over to them. I'm coming back either way—I'm going to be born very early in the new year, and I'll be ready to come home in the spring, and it's not negotiable. I've already been delaying this enough. I don't want to stay here not being in a body. I'm too bored. So, I'm picking out the perfect situation and the perfect way to transition and I'm putting the plan into action. I'm putting the plan in place.

"I want my parents to understand that no matter what, I'm coming back as a dog. When people see me, they're going to say, oh what a beautiful dog. Oh my gosh, he's so handsome. I want a high level of intelligence and I want an even higher level of athleticism. So, if they choose to have me in their life, that's wonderful, and if not, then I know that the perfect family is going to present themselves, but it's not negotiable for me. I need to have adventure. And if I don't come home to be with my family again, and by the way, let me just put this out there—I really feel that they can handle me—especially my dad. He still has a love for action and adventure. If my dad doesn't feel he can handle me, then I want to describe for you the perfect person. It would be a younger version of my dad. But I don't feel this is an issue. I feel like it's more of a mental state of him feeling like, I don't know if I'm going to be able to do this in 10 years. But I'll tell you right now, he will be able to. And when it's time for him to start winding down, it will also be time for me to start winding down. I still want a whole other decade together. In 10 or 12 years from now, he'll start feeling like he's old but he doesn't feel like that now. And I want to keep him young. If he doesn't feel like he can handle that, then I'm going to find another man who is athletic and strong and intelligent and empathetic and compassionate and strong and athletic." (He repeats those multiple times—he probably said it about five times actually). "And I want to have a life of adventure with him."

"My soul mate person isn't anyone else. It's my dad, but I also want this life of adventure. So, if it means that I just have to settle to be with someone who I don't have a deep soul mate connection with, so we can do all of these fun things, I guess that would be okay. These are all the things that I want to do."

"Ringo gives me a really strong feeling of someone who plans a cruise and they want to go on a cruise," Amanda told us. "They want to go scuba diving, jet skiing. They want to do all these things and their family says, you know I don't think we're going to go on this cruise and he says, 'Well, I'm still going with or without you. If I have to go parasailing by myself, so be it. I'll go with or without you because I signed up for these adventures. I would love for you to be there, but if you're not going to be there then one of the other solo passengers on the boat is going to have to go with me.' It's not about a soulmate connection with anybody else. He doesn't feel like he has another soulmate family. He feels like you guys are his soulmate family. But it's not negotiable for him.

"He's really stubborn. I don't remember him being this stubborn. As much as you're telling me, Kathy, that you guys are not sure you could handle this undertaking, so to speak, what he is showing me is very different. What he's showing me is that he feels as though, by coming back and by being this youthful dog, he is going to really match his dad's energy and they're going to both have this high level of strength and athleticism and this young strong man energy until 12 years from now and then they're both going to be like, 'Gosh I feel old. Do you feel old? Yeah, I feel old too, let's skip our hike today, let's just sit on the couch and relax. Let's just get a movie or watch TV and read a book.' He feels like he is ready for this life of adventure and more importantly he feels like his dad can handle it. So, what he's saying is, I'm coming back, and I'm going to leave it up to you if you decide to come and get me, and if you don't, I'm still having this adventure, and if you do, I'm very happy because I want to be with my family again."

Amanda asked George, "What do you have to say to this?"

"Well, it's tempting me to tell you the truth. That's part of the problem with this. You know, if you've ever loved a border collie, it's like loving a very beautiful woman, like my wife. There's a lot to it that's so desirable and there's a lot that comes with it. High maintenance is a word that comes to mind. But it does make me almost reconsider whether or not that is something I would do. I am still very active and plan on being very active and it's not that, it's just the whole picture of our lifestyle. We've been limited by Ringo in his old age. We wouldn't be limited by young Ringo in the same way. Part of it is that—I'm a dog trainer and I've gained so much knowledge and experience that I feel far better equipped to take on a puppy or a new dog than I ever have been before in my whole life. So, I think I could probably handle it quite well," he responded.

"I think it's something to consider," Amanda continued. "I've fostered many border collies. They actually remind me a lot of pit bulls in terms of their high energy and intensity and athleticism, so I know they are a lot to handle. But Ringo is very clear that he wants to be with you and he thinks that you could give him what he needs physically, emotionally, spiritually, energetically, and that he doesn't see a problem. He thinks you'll have a good twelve years, then you'll both begin to slow down and settle into that. He feels as though the two of you would be in very compatible energy. So, really, he's like, 'Here you are, the ball is in your court. I'll be ready to come home in the spring. Are you ready for me? Come and find me. If not, I'll catch you next lifetime.' With Ringo, very much in this communication it's like fire or ice. He's all energy, all out. He's all in on this idea. Honestly, this feels good to me. I feel good because I feel like it will give the two of you until March to consider what you're doing and then make the decision from there. Give yourself some time to marinate on it and let your heart guide you."

"I have a couple more questions around this," I said. "First of all, I'm wondering if he would consider coming back as a little bit smaller version of himself, so that he could hop up on the couch, on our laps, that kind of thing. And would he consider coming back as mostly black with some white this time? Those would be things that would be desirable to us. And, how would we find him?" I asked.

"Oh, that's never a question. They always find us. They always find us," Amanda said.

Amanda then asked him if he wanted to share some answers to our questions.

"'I already know what you're going to ask. Will I be a purse dog?' he asked and I told him, 'No, that was definitely not my question,'" Amanda said.

He said, "Yeah, because that was what you were imagining."

"Honey, I'm sorry, I misinterpreted your mom's question."

He asked, "Do you know what my answer would have been? Hell no! I might as well be a cat."

"So, I showed him again what the question was," Amanda said.

"Oh, would I be okay with being a little bit smaller?"

"Yeah, you wouldn't be quite as big and so maybe not as powerful, not as strong."

"You don't have to pitch me the idea, I was already planning on being 33 pounds. Is that too big?" Ringo asked.

"You're saying 33 pounds?"

And he answered, "Yeah, 33, sometimes 34, most of the time 33."

"'That's very specific,' I told him and he said, 'Well, that's how big I planned on being. Is that too big?' And I said, 'No, I don't think 33 is too big. I think your mom had more of like 25 pounds in mind.' But he insisted that he really wanted to be 33 pounds. I said, 'I'm sorry I'm laughing, but I've never heard such a clear, specific weight except once in my life and it was my own dog and he's exactly that weight to this day.'"

"Yeah, when you want what you want, you should get it," he said, "Well pitch the idea of 33 pounds to her and see if she likes that. I definitely don't want to be very large."

"I asked him how come and he explained his position on this," Amanda told us.

"Because I feel like it would be easier to do things a little bit easier if I'm smaller. Do you know what I mean by that? I want to make this clear for you, so you can understand me. As you get older, if you're heavier, and you're bigger, even if it's just muscle mass, it gets uncomfortable and it wears on your bones very heavily. So, I feel like I want to be smaller. I feel like it would be so much easier to not have that extra weight on my body to be carrying around. That's really the main reason."

"How about your color?" Amanda asked. "Do you have any specific plans on color?

He said, "I've really thought that over. I initially thought I would be all white but now I think, no. I just want to be back home, with my dad specifically. I would be okay being a different color. What do they want?"

"'Well your mom was thinking more black with some white,' and I pictured a border collie mostly black. He said, 'Oh, that's fine.' He shrugged it off like, that's nothing, that's not a big deal."

"That's not even a question. So, mostly black, small. Yeah, done and done. The first one isn't even a compromise because I already planned on being small," he told her.

Amanda continued to negotiate with Ringo, "Another thing that kind of concerns them is, how will they find you?"

And he said, "How will they find me? I'm coming home. What do they mean? They don't have to go out searching for me."

"Well, sometimes the process for people is scary and overwhelming," Amanda explained.

"No, I won't make it overwhelming for them. There are going to be a lot of people who are talking about me and excited about me coming back, even if they don't know it's me coming back," he said.

Amanda said, "I really don't understand that statement."

"You don't need to understand it, you just need to tell it to my parents. You're always trying to analyze everything."

"I'm sorry, I'm just trying to understand what I'm telling them so that I can help them understand."

"Just say it, and when I come home they're going to know that it's me coming home. They're going to recognize me. People are going to say, 'Oh, he's so cute, he kind of reminds me of Ringo.'"

"I get it. They don't have to worry about finding you."

"No, I promise they don't. The one thing that's most important to me, I just wish that more than anything else, when I come home, as soon as they introduce me to the home they say, 'Can you believe you're back here again? Can you believe that here we are, we're back here again?'"

"And he repeated it over and over and over," Amanda told us. "And I said, 'Honey, why are you repeating it like a mantra? Why are you saying it so many times?'"

"Because I'm going to be so happy to be back home, to be back with my family, to be back to have this whole new adventure ahead of me and I really want to make sure that they're saying that because it's not just that I want to be there, I want them to know I'm back. Do you understand what I'm saying to you?"

"Yeah. I do. I believe you want acknowledgment for not just being born into the world but specifically that it is YOU all over again."

"Yes, of course, of course I want to be acknowledged for being myself," he said.

"You're putting a lot of emphasis on that," Amanda told him.

"Well, it's important to me. I kind of feel a little bit guilty right now, because I've made it very nonchalant and I've shrugged about whether or not I come back to be with my parents again. I've said, 'Well, I'll come back either way, even if I don't come back with them.' But the truth of the matter is that isn't what I want at all. I don't want to relay that message so casually as if it doesn't really matter to me. I love my family so much. My mom is my heart, and my dad is my dude, and I want to be with them again. So, can you just really try to pitch that for me? And can you also just apologize because I shouldn't have been so nonchalant. But if they feel like they can't handle me, I won't hold a grudge. I won't be sad, but I want them to know how much I truly love them." He was very adamant about this.

"When we got Ringo, we didn't know anything about border collies," I told Amanda. "We made the mistake of getting him from a working farm, so he had this intense personality of a working dog. This time, we'd want a dog that is more of a companion dog rather than a working dog. So, our question for Ringo, would he be okay with that? And would it matter to him if he was female?"

"I told you in the beginning of this call that I was awakened by a dog in my dreams. Now that I fully feel Ringo's energy, I'm confident that it was him. He has definitely been pestering me to get his messages across. He's very disgruntled that it took this long," Amanda said.

"The question about working stock—that, for him, was very off-putting. I said, 'Being a working stock is off-putting?' He said, 'Yeah, because I'm very intense, right?' I said, 'Yes, honey, you're pushy and you're very intense. No offense but you're pretty demanding.'"

"Yeah, that's because I'm excited about coming home and I'm excited about getting out of here—I need to be in a body. I'm pretty intense right? Do you think that that's my soul?"

"I know it's your soul," Amanda said.

"Okay, now imagine pairing an already intense soul with an intense body. It's combustible. It felt like sometimes too much. Like my brain was like tick, tick, tick, tick, tick. I don't want that. I don't want that same level of high intensity. It's almost like adding fuel to the fire. So, no, I definitely don't want that. I want to be bred as a companion, a pet. I like the word pet because it means like, pet me."

"Okay, that's really cute, I'm definitely going to use that in the future," Amanda said.

"I want to be bred in a home. I want to be a pet. I want to be a family member. So, that's easy. It's not even a second thought, but I want to be really clear. I need to be born into a breeder's home. I don't want to be a shelter dog. I don't want to be a mutt. I want to come from a breeder who just loves Border Collies and they chose to have puppies because they love their family members, but I don't want to have to come back with this intensity." He had more to say.

He said, "And I want to talk about something else. When I come home, I want to make sure that they don't have a lot of worries."

"What do you mean worries?" Amanda asked.

"Well, worries about me. Worries about my body."

"He said that last time he felt like he was just so tired in his body and it felt like it was almost like carrying bags of bricks there was just so much baggage," Amanda told us.

"When I come home, I feel like I'm excited about coming home in a young puppy body but I'm afraid."

"Afraid of what?"

"Afraid of what's going to happen if I still am carrying around some of the baggage I had before."

"Honey, that doesn't happen. I think that's just a fear that you need to get out of your mind and leave behind," Amanda said. "You're not feeling that now, right?"

And he said, "No, but sometimes I think about it."

"Like the physical discomfort you were in?"

"Yes."

"You have plenty of time to let go of those bags before you are born," Amanda told him.

He replied, "Okay. It's just strange for me to think about being in such a little pain free body because I was so heavy before."

"I know, honey, but that's just a normal fear and you'll let it go."

Amanda continued, "He asked me if I had any advice on that and I said, 'Just don't think about it because it's not going to happen.' And he told me that was good!"

"Well then, when I come home, can they make sure that it's my job to just be always going somewhere with them? Wherever they go, I want to go. Especially if there's going to be anything at all where I'm breathing in fresh air. I don't need to go in stores. That's not my goal. I don't care about that at all. I just want to go places outside."

"He tells me that even if it's something as mundane as going to get the mail, or going to take out garbage he really wants to be like a shadow and I said, 'Okay, I got it.'"

"Can you tell me something else?" Ringo asked. "When I come home, can you make sure that wherever I go and people see me that they associate that my dad is, well, he's the dad? I want people to say, 'Oh, my gosh, he looks just like you.' People are going to see us and they're going to say, 'That's kind of weird, they sort of look alike.'"

"Ringo, I'm not sure what to do with that information. It's a little strange. I don't know what you want me to say," Amanda said.

"Well, just tell my dad that because when I come home, people are going to say that and I want him to know that it's my intention."

"Okay, but now moving to a different subject, how would you feel about being a girl? Is that something that appeals to you?"

"Of course, that appeals to me," Ringo told her.

Amanda asked him why he felt that way.

"Because I'm obsessed with my dad, right? And who more to be obsessed with their dad than a daddy's girl. I'm totally fine with that, that's completely on the table for me."

"I'm really surprised," Amanda said.

"Why are you surprised? Don't you feel like my energy is like everywhere my dad goes I want to be his shadow? And I just want to love my mom, but my bond isn't really going to be to her other than to just hang out with her here and there, but I'm really my dad's sidekick. Wouldn't you describe that as a daddy's girl? I'm totally fine with coming back as a girl. It's absolutely, completely on the table."

"He doesn't see his gender as having the relevance that we humans give it. A lot of animals are very predominantly male or female. Ringo's energy is just like athletic, adventurous, intense and I wouldn't really put a gender on that energy. But he describes himself as a daddy's girl and wanting to look like dad which is... I've seen dogs say things like that, but I've always thought that they visually looked alike. I can't imagine how George and a border collie are going to look alike visually. But maybe their energies are going to be so similar or complementary that, well, we're just going to have to see. It was just so random. I had to tell you though because he really wanted you to know," Amanda said.

"Have I ever met you, George? The way I picture you through your animals is being rather fair skinned, maybe German ancestry or something of that nature. And when I picture a border collie, I can't tie my vision of you with a border collie. Maybe I'm wrong and maybe you do have similar hair and color of a border collie. I don't see it, but he says that people are going to say that you two look so much alike."

George then said to Amanda, "I have to tell you something. Back when the covid thing started, I started growing a beard. I've got grey hair but I've got a white and black beard. And I am a fair-skinned German."

"Wow, George. Wow! Wow! Wow! That's crazy. That makes me really happy because I was like, this is so weird, so random. I love it when I feel like I'm nuts and I get validated.

"So, Ringo says the word pet with a lot of emphasis. I would say when you hear about the breeder, you should make certain they are breeding for companionship, not for working dogs."

"We want to let you know that, contrary to when we first spoke, we've decided we want to get a border collie now," George told Amanda.

"Good! Oh, that makes me so happy. I don't even have words to express how I'm about to cry. That makes me so happy because this is what he really feels is just meant to be. That he is really meant to grow, with you especially George, over the next decade and just have these wonderful adventures in exploring life and nature together."

"Would you take a minute to tell him that for us it's important that he is pointing himself in the direction of a 33 pound, primarily black female border collie?" I asked Amanda.

"Of course, of course. Oh, I have goosebumps. I'm so happy. I told him I'm so very happy for him and that you just want to make confirmation that here are the must haves: 33 lbs., predominantly black, female, family pet, spring."

"Yes, that all of those things are check, check, check, check. Can you also make sure that you're emphasizing the word, family pet. Pet is the word, that's what I want to be," Ringo told her.

Amanda told us, "I feel like that's how the puppies are going to be advertised or that's going to be a word that is used in the description or a word someone says." She further explained, "So, sometimes when I'm communicating with pets, I'll see a word that is highlighting or if there's a color for me that is very significant. When I'm talking to Ringo, the word pet keeps coming up and it's in CAPS and it's very bold, so that is going to have some significance in how you identify him," she said.

"You'll know when the time is right. You'll be guided. Just listen to your inner voice which will be influenced by Ringo's voice. You know, it's just the way that the Universe or God or the Angels or however you want to phrase it, works everything out. It's just perfect."

Ringo chimed in again to say, "I really don't want to be in a body and moving around until it's nice and warm outside."

Amanda said, "Honey, you live in Southern California, isn't it always warm even when it's the coldest?"

But he said, "No, I don't want to feel a chill. I don't like the idea of that, especially because I feel like I'm going to be small and not have a lot of body fat to keep me warm. I'm not going to be back in a body and ready to go home to my family until spring."

"I got it," Amanda told him. "So, the second part of the question is, in the spring, will you be such a young puppy that you'll be, you know, eight weeks old? Or 10 weeks old when they get you? Or will you be a little bit older, seven to eight months old?"

And he said, "No, I want to share my whole life with them from the moment that I can."

"He doesn't want to experience even the slightest chill in the air. He wants to be born when it's nice and warm and you can go outside and start doing stuff right away. He doesn't want to feel like it's too chilly for such a little girl. He definitely is going to be born in a home, with an at home breeder that is family-oriented and you will not meet him until the spring.

"Everything just really feels like it's a go. It feels like a train. You can't push a train off its tracks. It feels like this is an absolute definite. Like it's written in stone."

Amanda finished by saying, "I'm so excited. I just feel like this is absolutely meant to be. He's meant to be back home. You know, we may have human doubts, but it doesn't matter. This is meant to be, and you'll see later how perfect his presence is in your life and what a saving grace he is going to be for you."

CHAPTER THIRTY-SEVEN
Matty Misses Ringo.

Matty was in need and so, of course, we called Amanda.

"I'm sensing Matty might be struggling in some way. He's gained weight, but not eating much more. He's itching like crazy, and his lumps are starting to grow back," I told her.

"And I want to know how he feels about Ringo coming back as a puppy, and how much he enjoys going to the park," George chimed in.

"I asked him how he was feeling, what was going on, and if there was anything he wanted to share with me," Amanda told us. "He showed me that his 'little lumps' were coming back. He said, 'I feel them again. They're more embarrassing than uncomfortable.' He showed me that it's very close to one calendar year of the time that he had lumps in the past. You had them removed almost exactly one calendar year ago? He said, 'Yes, it's my anniversary with the bumps, do you understand?' I said, 'Yes, honey, I understand.'"

"There's nothing wrong. I don't have anything wrong with me so these lumps are pointless. It's not doing anything for the inner part of my body."

"I'm very glad to hear that you don't feel any pain or discomfort with them," Amanda told him. "He said, he has no pain but he feels embarrassment," she explained to us.

Matty continued, "Will you please tell my parents there doesn't need to be another appointment with, you know, the doctor taking them away? It would be pointless. Even if you get rid of them again, they're going to come back."

"Okay, sweetheart, I'll tell them," Amanda replied. "Now, can you tell me a little bit about how you're feeling?"

"I'm feeling tired. I feel like my body is a little bit more tired."

"Internally or externally?"

"Internally."

"So it feels like things are moving slower internally? Does that make you feel sluggish on the outside?" Amanda asked.

"No, not sluggish. I just feel like I'm getting old. I know that I'm not that old, but I feel like my body is starting to slow down."

"What he means by this is that he's not saying that he's feeling lazy and tired, physically. What he's saying is that he feels like his body is slower to function and slower to move things around, like his metabolism is maybe slowing down, maybe it's just taking a little longer for everything to function. It doesn't feel problematic to me. It feels like there are no red flags in our communication up until now," Amanda explained.

"I asked him if there is something I'm missing? Is there something that you're not telling me?"

"Yeah, one thing that I want to tell you is that I feel like I'm thirsty but when I'm drinking it's not quenching my thirst."

"He is showing me a feeling of almost being, not dehydrated, but I'm wondering if it has to do with his blood sugar. I'm not sure," Amanda continued.

"And he said, 'I want to show you overall how I'm feeling.' He is showing me that, though his appetite is not gone, his food doesn't have the same appeal as it normally had. That's how he's looking at food. He's feeling like he's thirsty. Even if he's drinking, he still feels thirsty like he can't quite quench that thirst. And he's feeling a little bit of discomfort in his back."

Matty went on to tell Amanda, "I just feel like things are starting to hit the brakes a little bit. But I do feel like I'm getting old. I don't want to admit that, but that's how my body feels. But with all that being said, when they get a puppy, I feel like that's going to bring back life to my body."

"Why do you say that?" she asked him.

"Because we're all waiting for him to come back. And we all miss him so much. He generated so much energy in our house. I feel like my body is in line with my spirit. I feel like I've had a really hard time since Ringo passed because we were such a pack. The three of us were just.... well, when you thought of one, you thought of all of us." Amanda says, "I'm going to cry." "And because he had such a special bond with my parents, everybody just feels lonely. Everybody feels sad. So, I need for him to come back."

"Are you not well bonded with your other buddy?" Amanda asked him.

"Well, we all love each other, we're family, and when one of the family members is missing, especially someone we saw as the leader, or like the older brother, not leader in a dominant way, but the elder, that's the word, the elder. I really need him to come back and I really need this young, youthful energy. I feel like my body, everything is slowing down, all of these things I'm experiencing, they are all symptoms of my sadness."

"Wow, honey, I didn't realize you were so sad." Amanda told him.

"Yes, as time passes, it's harder because I realize the emptiness I feel without him. And the anticipation of him coming back as a puppy is wearing on me. I need that. I need some youthful energy. I need it to shift things a little bit. Everything is getting harder for me because my body is naturally aging. Because my mind is sad, that's making everything speed up. The process of aging is speeding up."

"I understand. Is there anything I can do in the meantime?"

"Tell my parents not to worry about me. Please don't take me to the vet and start nitpicking me because no matter what I'm experiencing, I'll be feeling better when we have a puppy. And the weakness in my body is something that is going to happen regardless of whether you put me through treatments and medications. And then one symptom leads to another symptom and then there's the domino effect of medication. I just want to be. And so, can you tell them that that's the most important thing to me?"

"Of course, yes, I will share all of those things with them," she assured Matty.

Amanda continued, "So, what Matty is telling me is that a lot of the symptoms, the things that I'm feeling within him, could be that it's just how he's feeling today. He feels like the best thing to do is leave him be, get the puppy, let that pep him up. This is all part of aging for Matty, but it's also part of stress and loss. Does that make sense to you, Kathy and George?"

We answered, "Yes."

"Another thing we worry about is that he seems to have skin problems. He's always itching," I told Amanda.

"I asked him to share with me about his symptoms of eczema, and he said, 'Can I take you back for a minute?' And I said, 'Sure.'"

"I want to tell you that sometimes I feel this—and it's like all of a sudden, out of nowhere, I feel this extreme fatigue like, oh gosh, I'm so tired. I don't want to take another step. I want to lay down right here. And it only lasts about 10 seconds. And then I can get up and I can walk again. It starts in my shoulders but the extreme exhaustion is really in my back end."

"He explained that he's so afraid that if he's walking he's just going to collapse or that he'll just lay down really quickly. Or he's not able to get up as quickly as he wants to because he says he feels like an overall body exhaustion that is stemming from—I don't know—I feel like it's something that happened early in his life. You may not have even had him, but he had some kind of nerve damage and all of a sudden, because he's aging, because his body is getting old, well, it's not like nerve pain, it's almost like paralysis. It's just like, oh, oh, I can't walk right now. My muscles, my nerves, everything is in motion to go, but I need to just stay here," Amanda said.

"I asked him, 'Sweetheart, so when you have this extreme fatigue, is there anything that's causing it?'"

"No, absolutely not. It happens out of the clear blue, out of nowhere. It's not that often, but it is something that happens."

Amanda continued, "The reason that I'm telling you this is that if you call him to come and he doesn't come right away, it's not that he's ignoring you, and he has no hearing issues. It's that his body, in that moment, is feeling like he just can't get up and move. It feels almost numb, like paralysis. But it only lasts about 10 seconds and then he's fine. I don't know if it's a circulation issue. I don't know if it's a neurological issue. But he's showing me that it's stemming from something that happened in the past. He's saying, come on, let me take you back, and he's rewinding a great deal, but I don't see what he's rewinding to. I just see that something happened in the past and he still has that imprint in his body and because he's getting old and starting to feel tired, and because he feels like he's entering his senior years, his body is just not working. I know that this sounds like I'm kind of talking all over the place, but are you following me at all? Do you understand what he's telling you?"

"We're absolutely following you on this," I told her. "To fill you in—he had an injury when he was about three-years-old. And he was paralyzed in his hind end."

"Wow, how long did that last for?"

"Well, long story short, the vets told us there was nothing they could do and they wanted to euthanize him. We found a wonderful chiropractor who adjusted him and within 24 hours he was walking, within 48 hours he was running around the backyard. And it stemmed from his neck being out of alignment, but it affected him in his back end," I informed her.

"That's interesting because that's exactly where I feel it in my own body. I feel like it's starting like around my shoulders and around my collarbone area and then it kind of leads back and then I feel like I can't get up because I have needles and it's just numb from the bottom down. That's very interesting. Wow! That's so interesting."

"I want you to ask him something about this. The chiropractor taught us to do a tractioning on his neck. And honestly, we kind of don't do that anymore because he seems fine. So, would you ask him if he remembers that traction and if that helps him and if he wants us to do it again?" I asked Amanda.

"Yes, I'll ask him that. Thank you for validating that. It felt so weird that it was starting in my shoulders."

She told us that Matty said, "Yes I remember that technique."

"'Does it help?' I asked him," Amanda said. "And he said, 'Yes, it helps a great deal.' And he showed me a number 10 and I said, 'Oh you're so cute. So, you mean it's a 10 out of 10?' And he said, 'Yes, that much.' I said, 'You're so adorable that you showed me a 10 out of 10. I don't think I've ever seen a dog do that. It's so human-like. So, you think that will make a difference?'"

"Yes, that will make a difference with that one thing I'm showing you and I want them to be clear in understanding that when I'm feeling this moment of numbness, I don't want them to think I'm ignoring them."

"Is this something that has been happening often lately or are you almost laying the foundation for the future?"

"It's been happening, but it's more so me laying down the foundation for the future. I don't want them to start worrying that my hearing is going. No hearing issues whatsoever on the board. So, if they see me ignoring them, I need them to understand why."

"I asked him, 'Can I tell you what I believe is happening?' And he said, 'Sure.' 'I think that you're still really sad about Ringo and the anticipation of him coming is driving you nuts and the fact that he's not there is making you crazy. I feel like there hasn't been a whole lot of positive change happening in your life in a while and that's a problem for you emotionally. And I feel like all the things that were bothering you before, whether it was your neck or whether it was your lower end being numb or paralyzed, or whether it's your itching. Everything is coming back to the forefront now because you're in some emotional distress. Does that sound right to you?'"

"Yes, it does."

"I want to explain to your parents that the issues with you being thirsty, not being as hungry as normal, everything sort of slowing down, I don't believe that it is disease. I believe it could just be that you are feeling emotional. Is that correct?"

"Yeah, it is."

"He's emotional, and so all of the physical pain he has ever had is coming back to the forefront. I didn't realize how hard of a time he's having without Ringo there. But he saw Ringo as such a safe place and like a protector of the house. Without that, there's maybe a fear, an anxiety? It's more than just sadness. He's lacking that feeling of security that he once had. It's really kind of like a house of cards. Everything is falling apart because he doesn't have that security and it's just knocked it all over," Amanda said.

"This wave of sadness and grief overcomes me to the point where I could easily bawl my eyes out for the next 20 minutes. Kathy and George, I'm feeling very emotional and as an animal communicator, I am having a hard time containing the sadness that I'm feeling from him. So, everything that he's experiencing, I really see to be all because of this root of Ringo being gone."

Amanda then said to Matty, "I want to give you a couple of tools to use before Ringo comes home. One thing is, I'm going to mention to your mom and dad to do something new and different that they haven't done before, something exciting so that it could shift the energy and get you really excited. I asked him, 'Is there anything that you particularly love the most? Do you like going for walks much? Do you want to go to meet people? What do you love the most that would make you really excited?' He showed me that it's not walking somewhere and seeing people that gets him really riled up. It's—if you could take him for a car ride and take him to somewhere where there are a lot of people and they could see him. For him that would almost be like his love language, so to speak. It's the car ride going somewhere fun. That would make him feel better while we're all waiting."

Amanda then told us, "It would benefit everyone to change the energy of the house and get more excited in talking about how fun it's going to be with a puppy coming. It should be a daily occurrence that you talk about that. Give him that to look forward to. Almost like a countdown like, oh my gosh, it's only this amount of weeks. Oh, my goodness, it's going to be so fun. You're going to have a puppy to play with. Even though it's going to be a puppy, it's going to make you feel so safe. And just talk to him like you would a five-year-old child if you had a baby coming in. He needs to have that shifted energy.

"I feel like nothing is really wrong with him other than emotions. The problem is, he has a broken heart. He has a heavy heart. Does that make sense to you?"

"Yes, it does," I replied. "I've been sensing his heaviness and not quite knowing what it was and that's why we wanted you to check in with him. What you're saying makes perfect sense. Matty is a sensitive little soul."

Amanda told us a story about a Bishon Frishee rescue she took in from a shelter. "This dog was so lethargic, seeming like she was on her way out. I took her home because I wanted her to be in a home, surrounded by love during her last days. As soon as I got her home, within days, she was up, running around, playing with my very large pitbull. I thought, she's got spunk, this girl. She survived. She was happy and healthy and she loved me, so I decided I was going to keep her. That was eight years ago and she's an awesome dog.

"I recently took in a cat of a terminally ill little girl. The poor child was on chemo. She had already lost all her hair. She was very ill. They were going to give the cat to the shelter but they were all out of space so, the shelter was going to have to euthanize her. I told the mom and the little girl, I'll take the cat and I'll give her a really loving home, I promise. It was a very emotional experience. I brought the kitten home. The kitten wasn't terribly well. She said that she just wanted to be with her girl. But they couldn't keep the kitten because of the immune problems that come with chemo. The girl had become allergic to the kitten. So, I explained to the kitten that she couldn't stay with her, but that I would give her the best home that I could. She was okay for a few weeks. She slept with Fiona, my dog, every night. And then the kitten decided, about six weeks later, that this wasn't for her. She was meant to be with this other little girl. I thought, based on my communication with the kitten, the little girl was probably close to crossing over. The kitten said she just wanted to go and be with her and even if she could only be with her in spirit, that's better than not at all and the kitten got, within hours, very, very sick. I rushed her to the emergency vet. I wasn't listening to what she said—'I want to leave.' I thought, I don't care if I have to spend my last dollar, I want to help heal this kitten. So, of course, the vet did everything they could. They kept her on fluids, but two days later she passed away.

"I came home and I explained to my dogs that Flower wouldn't be coming back. Fiona was so sad and she said, 'But I was healing her,' and I said, 'Honey, I know, but she wanted to go be with her person, and Fiona said, 'But I was sleeping with her every night and I was keeping her warm and I was telling her how great life can be and that I was also very sick like her and that I was going to heal her. And I was giving her strength and energy every night.' And I said, 'I'm so sorry, Fiona. There's nothing I can do, honey, she passed away. She's gone. She's not coming back. She's with her person now.'" Amanda went on.

"My dog got so sick within days of the kitten passing away. She got two really bad eye infections. She couldn't even open her eyes. I was giving her medicine and eye drops and eye wash and it just wasn't working. And so, I asked, 'Fiona, honey, what is wrong?' Because I did everything I knew how to do. And she said, 'I just don't want to see that she's not here.' She had manifested an infection in her eyes. It took a lot of talking to her and patience and communication and she's fine now. That was only a few days ago, but when animals are so in an emotional space, the things that they create in their bodies are unbelievable. What my dog did was so symbolic of her not wanting to see the reality of her friend being gone," Amanda said.

"So, when I connected to Matty just now, it wasn't one thing, it was everything that he had experienced in his past that was uncomfortable. He's now bringing it all back to physically show you how he's emotionally feeling."

CHAPTER THIRTY-EIGHT
Finding Ringo: The Search Begins.

The search began. We had our very specific checklist, co-created by me, George and Ringo. We began searching for a breeder who bred a line of dogs that met our "must haves."

We were looking for a companion dog, a pup who would be our pet, not a working dog. She would be a female, on the smaller size, black and white. Our perfect breeder would be in love with the breed and a meticulous at-home breeder. Our perfect breeder would love all of their dogs as though they were each a precious gift delivered to their care and keeping. Our breeder would be highly discriminating about who would get the privilege of adopting one of their babies. And our perfect breeder would be highly sensitive when told the story of Ringo, our soul dog, who would be returning to us in the body of one of their puppies.

After an extensive search, we found them. Orshi and Frank Horvath, founders of Overdrive Border Collies. They were, indeed, our perfect breeders. And an added bonus was that they lived only twenty minutes away. After looking at breeders from all over the country, it was a definite bonus that they were geographically close.

Orshi and Frank had been breeding border collies for fifteen years. They had carefully developed a line of dogs with beautiful physical qualities, and a temperament that was calm and loving. Their dogs are beautiful, intelligent, energetic but not frenetically so. They were breeding dogs to be the perfect companion dog. *The perfect pet.*

Many of their dogs have gone on to place highly in the ring for conformity, obedience, herding, and agility. This line of dogs seemed to be perfection. Beautiful, loving, calm, highly intelligent, and athletically skilled. We made an appointment to meet Orshi and Frank and their dogs.

When we arrived at their home, we were ushered to the backyard where we sat on the ground to meet a few of their dogs. We got to meet three of their breeding females. All were stunningly beautiful and very sweet. We were greeted with lots of licks, wags, and snuggles. There was a puppy amongst them. A male, about 12 weeks old, ready to be placed in his forever home. It was hard not to just scoop that little boy up and claim him as our own, but we knew the timing wasn't right.

Orshi and Frank were so friendly and welcoming. They listened to our story of Ringo's reincarnation with earnest engagement. They got it. They were on board with the timing. It was then that they introduced us to Cherry, one of their prize bitches. She was gorgeous! She was from Hungary and had been bred by artificial insemination, using the semen of Levi, a prize male from Australia. They had the semen shipped to them, bred Cherry with it, and were awaiting confirmation that she was, indeed, pregnant. If pregnant, her puppies would be born at the perfect time for them to be ready to find their homes in early springtime. My gut told me that this was Ringo's litter. I was sure of it. We gave them a deposit and went home to await the text letting us know that Cherry was pregnant. Within a week, we got the good news. Cherry was indeed pregnant and her puppies would be due at the end of January.

Now it was a waiting game. How many puppies would Cherry have? Would she produce female puppies? Which one of those pups would be the physical expression of our precious Ringo's soul? How would we know?

After about a month, Orshi did an ultrasound and learned that there were likely four or five puppies. It was impossible to tell what sex they were, but we were hopeful that with that many puppies at least one would be a female. We waited patiently for the birth. Finally, finally, on January 23rd, four adorable puppies were born. Two males and two females.

Oh, my God!!! We were beyond excited. *Our Ringo boy has come back to us.* Now it was a waiting game. It would be nine long weeks before she would be old enough to come home. We had some work to do to prepare. It was time to get baby gates, an appropriately sized crate, toys and balls, a tiny collar and leash. And it was time to choose a name for our new baby.

The first name given to our little girl was "Dot Girl." This was her newborn puppy name, given at birth by Orshi and Frank because she had a little black dot on the right side of her white snout. These baby names are given to tell the puppies apart when they are tiny. Though an adorable moniker, we needed to choose something more permanent.

We chose the name Nina. First of all, our favorite (current) mountain biker is a Swiss cyclist named Nino Schurter. He has a myriad of awards for being the fastest and most skilled men's racer. And, he's just an all-around nice guy. Because mountain biking was such a big part of our bond with Ringo, we thought it would be nice to name this little girl the female version of Nino. The other reason we chose this name was to honor Nina Simone, the singer and civil rights activist whom we both admire. Nina would be this little girl's name.

Now, it was time to tell Matty, Pinto, and Tinker that Ringo was coming home and ask them how they would feel about having a new puppy in our family.

CHAPTER THIRTY-NINE

A New Puppy? Whatcha think?

We called Amanda to check in with our crew and to let them know about Ringo coming home in the body of Nina. We wanted to get a reading as to how they were feeling about adding a puppy to our family.

We started with Tinker. Here's what Tinker said:

"I feel like I've found my voice. Remember how afraid I was? I felt like I had some really big shoes to fill. Now, I feel like my shell has hardened and I feel safe. I feel really safe. I'm feeling secure in myself. I feel brazen. It feels really fantastic. I'm proud of myself. I feel like I've grown more in the past six months than I've grown in my entire life."

Amanda explained, *"When Solo was with Tinker, there was a feeling that Solo was always front and center. Tinker could always be in a safe space. Now, what Tinker feels is like if a woman had gotten out of a long marriage where she was completely taken care of. Now, Tinker has to learn to do everything on her own. She feels liberated and independent."*

Amanda then asked about Matty. Tinker had been growling at Matty and chasing him out of rooms. Amanda asked her if she thought she may be being a little aggressive with Matty and Tinker said, *"No, it's all fun and games. He enjoys it. He's having a good time. He's not really afraid of me."*

Amanda explained, *"It's like Tom and Jerry. They're just having a good time."*

Tinker said, *"Matty is not really afraid of me. He understands very well that I'm coming into my own. I wouldn't say he's humoring me or patron-*

izing me, but I wouldn't disagree with those words either. Matty is not afraid. I'm just establishing boundaries. It's all healthy. We're developing a healthy friendship. Don't rag on me about it, okay?"

Amanda asked, "What about a puppy? I've heard many times over that a puppy is coming. Show me what it looks like from your point of view."

Tinker responded. "That looks really different than the way my parents are showing me. I believe that when my mom is projecting the images of having a puppy, it looks like a joy, but a chaotic experience too."

"To Tinker, this is a little frightening," Amanda told us.

"I feel pretty excited about it though. I feel like I'm getting old, around 14," Tinker told her. "I'm starting to feel muscle strain, a little weakness. I feel like having a puppy will give me some youth back. But this puppy needs to know that I am not to be messed with, so, expect me to have some strong boundaries. It's very different than my relationship with Matty. I want the puppy to understand that she can't play with me. She'll have strong teeth and she'll hurt me. So, if I'm a little bit too sassy or fierce with a puppy, it's just me saying I've finally found my voice and I'm not to be messed with." She went on to ask Amanda, "Are you proud of me?"

Amanda responded with, "Yes, honey. I'm very proud of you."

Amanda went on to tell us, "Having a puppy to 'boss around' will feel good to her and make her feel young. Tinker's picking up on more of the worse and less of the joy. She feels, from Kathy, the fear that this is going to be work instead of that the puppy is going to be joy."

"It's interesting that you're picking up on this and that it's my energy because I feel like it's more George's energy," I replied. "He has been nonstop, 24-hrs a day, thinking about the work he's going to have to do with this puppy. I've been thinking that the puppy is going to be fun, but the burden of all the work is on his shoulders." I turned to George. "I don't know, why don't you talk about it, honey," I asked him.

"Great observation, Amanda, because there will be a lot of things that Tinker will be exposed to: baby gates, crates being moved around, audio clips of sounds like sirens, and things to help socialize the puppy," George said. "The energy in the house is clearly going to be different than the calm things that are in her experience now. That's going to be an adjustment for everyone, but especially for Tinker because she's so sensitive."

"Wow, George, that is so surprising," Amanda responded. "I felt so sure that it was Kathy putting it out there. I completely had that backwards. To Tinker, it brings about more a feeling of anxiety than excitement or joy. I don't think there's anything you can do to change that because you're being sensible.

So, here's how it is: George is playing over the loudspeaker about how the changes are going to be in the house. This feels very anxiety-producing to Tinker because, Kathy, you're not putting out the opposite energy. Maybe you're thinking, oh, it's going to be fun, it's going to be a great time, but you're not playing it over the loudspeaker. I would love to see you spend a few minutes a couple of times a day intentionally putting out how wonderful it is going to be to have that energy in the house, and how wonderful it's going to be to have that part of your family back again, how spiritually nurturing it's going to be. And sit with her while you do this. Have her with you while you're doing this so that she can feel that calm space."

"I want to say something that may be even a surprise to George," I said. "But I may be projecting some anxiety too because sometimes, when George talks about all the problems we'll have to face, all the things we'll have to do, all the precise things we'll have to do to make sure this puppy is going to be raised right, I start to think, gosh, is this even going to be fun? Is it going to be a sweet experience or is it going to be taxing for everybody? I might be putting that out because I'm feeling that sometimes."

"It's not the puppy itself as much as it's the shift in the energy of the house that makes Tinker anxious," Amanda replied.

"Yes, I get that," I answered.

"Here's the thing about a puppy who is being reincarnated. They already have the blueprint of who they are, what they're supposed to be, so the training is a world of difference between them and any other puppy. They remember a lot of things. You'll see that she will learn things so quickly. You'll show her things and she'll get it. It's just like refreshing her memory. This will be the experience of Ringo returning, relearning. So, I hope that will calm you a little."

We then turned our attention to Pinto. George asked Amanda, "Please ask Pinto if he feels like he's going to be going from #1 to #2. I just want him to feel like he'll never go to #2 and he's going to be okay."

Amanda talked with Pinto and returned to us:

"He understands. He said, 'Can I show you how excited I am?' (Amanda laughed) I wasn't expecting so much emotion and adrenaline and so much depth.) I said, 'There is a lot of emotion coming in with Ringo's return.'"

Pinto said, "I know. There's so much."

(Amanda had to pause because she was very emotional about this; she was actually crying).

She asked Pinto, "Why is there so much emotion coming through? It's excitement, it's joy, it's almost bittersweet. There is so much emotion coming through, so much intensity, it's tugging at my heartstrings so much. Why am I feeling so much?"

Pinto replied, "It's because Ringo's return is so important for my family. It's so monumental. It's like the key that unlocks everything. The key that unlocks the deepest spirituality. It is the deepest spiritual space. It's like the rearing of a newly born child. It's the most miraculous thing my family is going to experience. And also, Ringo is deeply, deeply missed, and missing us tremendously. After his physical death, Ringo was coming in every day and saying, 'I just can't wait to come back.' Ringo would touch the walls and say, 'I miss this space so much. I miss my family. I miss the feeling of the thickest love in the air I've ever felt anywhere in the universe. The trust, the love, the compassion, the mutual respect. This is so rare. It's such a gem. I can't wait to come back and be in these walls again.'"

"Wow, Pinto!! Pinto said that Ringo told him over and over, 'I want to be the embodiment of the perfect dog. I can't wait to come back and be with my family. I can't wait to come back to be with you.' "Wow, Ringo said that?" Amanda asked Pinto.

"Yes, all the time, and I am so looking forward to his return. I know that means me moving over, but it doesn't mean me stepping down. Part of me is going to miss the undivided attention I get, but the greater part of me is so looking forward to being an older sibling. Teaching and learning. Learning patience. Sharing so much gratitude. I feel like there are so many soul lessons in this journey for me right now. I feel like I have so much more soul growth ahead of me than I've ever had behind me. It's about the expansion of love, not the separation of it. Please tell my dad that I'm not going to be envious. I'm not going to be jealous. I know that love is about sharing and that love is unconditional in this house. I have so many emotions about Ringo coming back."

(Amanda paused again, to cry).

"There is so much excitement, so much joy that it takes my breath away. I'm enjoying every moment here and now, and I'm enjoying the journey. I know that things are going to shift and change. I know that my parents are going to love me forever, no matter what. I also know that I'm going to get a fraction of the attention and energy that I get now. I know that I'm not going to be first anymore, but that's okay, that's okay, that's okay. I'm not unrealistic. I'm willing to move over and share the love because this is healing for all of us. This is the journey that we're on and I feel humbled that I get to be a part of it. I feel like I've grown up so much spiritually and I know that this is going to be multiplied and I'm ready for it," Pinto told her.

"The amount of emotion that I got really took me by surprise," Amanda told us. "I wasn't expecting for Pinto to be so mature. I was moved to tears numerous times during a three-minute conversation. It took me on such a high: the feeling of love and gratitude. This is different than a child having a younger sibling. I'm going to tell you another story to use as an example."

She told us about her husband who was a tremendous support for her. He told her that he knew he could never be number one. "He knew that my work with animals was the most important thing to me. And he was right. After about six years of marriage, I told him I think he would be happier if he met someone who would put him first. And why don't we take a break. He was so upset and so hurt, but about a year later, he met a woman who was crazy about him. I went to the wedding. It was sad. It was bittersweet to see him with someone else who could give him the love that I never could have given him. That's how I feel now when I hear Pinto say, 'I know I'm not going to be number one anymore, but I'm so grateful that I get to be a part of this monumental journey for our family.'"

"It's so emotional for Pinto, but it's so selfless. I keep hearing, on repeat, 'I know that I'm not going to be first, but that's okay. I know I'm going to feel left out, but that's okay. I know I'm going to be feeling moments of sadness or abandonment, but that's okay. It feels like this is a true definition of love. I know I'm going to be losing a bit, but that's okay because it's for the greater good of our family, and it's for the greater good of Ringo.' This is just really not what I was expecting from Pinto at all. It's probably the deepest, most emotional conversation I've ever had with any of your animals. There was a lot of depth," Amanda said.

"I asked Pinto if there was anything going on with him physically that was making him more emotional," Amanda told us.

"Not at all; please don't undermine my emotions. Don't you know what a big deal this is? Do you understand how much my life is going to shift and change? Do you understand how monumentally different every waking hour, and even every sleeping hour is going to be?" Pinto replied.

"Yes, I do."

"Then don't undermine my emotions by trying to make it something physical. Thank you for being my voice."

"Thank you so much for letting me be your voice, that's probably the nicest thing any animal has said to me."

"Can you tell my parents how much I love them and how grateful I am? Tell my mom how much I love spending quality time with my mom, just cuddled up and doing nothing, and how much I love doing everything with my dad, especially anything active."

Amanda then told us, "I'd like for you two to do a little something small, something special, with Pinto every day. Just two or three minutes each day. Just make it your intention and purpose that each of you do something special for him. There was so much bittersweet emotion. It would mean the world to me, as Pinto's voice, if you would make sure to do something for Pinto, just for him."

(As I, Kathy, remembered our first conversation with Pinto and what a little self-centered, immature pup he was, it strikes me how much he had grown up. We might have expected these deeply personal words of wisdom coming from Matthew, but not Pinto. I was rather blown away.)

We turned to Matty. Amanda said, "He is such a drastically different energy. His voice is far less emotional, just more logical. I asked him, 'So, Matty, how are things going? I heard that you're getting chased by a cat. Is that true?'"

He said, "Yes, but you know it's not really a big deal. I'm just kind of having fun. She messes with me a little bit, and I let her think that she's messing with me. She chases me and you know what I do? I run. But I'm not really scared. You know that she's a cat, right? You know that a cat can't really hurt a dog, right? It makes her feel good, so I let her have it. She doesn't have a lot because she's a cat. She can't do fun stuff. She's limited."

"Limited physically or mentally?" Amanda asked him.

"You know, they can't do as much. They're limited. They're cats."

"Then I asked him how he was doing." Amanda told us.

"I'm really good. You know we're getting a puppy, right? Do you know how much I love puppies? I love them so much. They're so cute. They're so fun, and they smell really good and you get to tell them stuff. Sometimes they listen, sometimes they don't, but either way it's going to be fun."

"But are you feeling nervous, jealous, sad?"

"No! Why would I be feeling jealous? I'm excited. I get to have fun. I get to chase someone around. They get to chase me. They get to learn. We get to grow together. It's going to be awesome. I'm really looking forward to this."

"So, Matty, I'm not getting any emotional baggage from you. Is there anything you're feeling that you might want to vent?"

Matty said, "No, why would I want to... wait, is the puppy going to eat my food?"

"Well, maybe sometimes," Amanda admitted.

"Well, then I'll vent about that. How much is he going to eat my food?"

"Well, sometimes when puppies are eating they don't have very good manners and they eat the other dog's food, but your mom and dad will help with that."

Matty said, "Well, that's the one thing I want to vent about. I really prefer that the puppy doesn't eat my food but other than that, I don't have any complaints."

"So, I told him, 'Your dad wants to talk about how proud he is of you and how you'll be his training assistant. Do you have anything you want to say about that?' Matty said, 'No, I feel happy.' 'Well, then do you have anything else you want to say?'"

"What do you want to hear?" Matty asked her. "I just told you. I don't have anything heavy. I keep feeling like you want me to say something heavy, but I don't have anything heavy. I feel happy, I feel ready, I feel like moving forward. I'm excited that Ringo is coming home. This is going to be a fun experience. Life is great."

"I'm glad this isn't the first time I've ever spoken with Matty because this feels very generic, like there is not a whole lot of depth to it. It's just, life is great, having a puppy is going to be great, please don't eat my food, what else do you want to hear? Everything is rosy. There is just a happy simplicity. Optimism. Nothing but joy," she told us.

"Matty was so depressed over missing Ringo. Now that that's out of the way, there is no more heaviness and he can return to being happy little Matty. Clear skies ahead."

We asked her a question about the next step in bringing our puppy home. We explained that the breeder makes the choice as to which female pup we get. We told her a little about the breeder, what we knew about the lineage, etc. And we asked, "So, what do we do now? Should we talk to the pup before she comes home? After she comes home? What do you advise?"

"There's really nothing to do but trust that the Universe will handle the details and that everything is divinely guided. If I were in your shoes, I would just be puppy proofing my house. There's really no point to do a communication beforehand. I'm not a big proponent of just checking in really often. Do I feel it necessary to check in with Ringo or Nina before she comes home? No. What is she going to say? I'm coming home. I'm excited. Do you really need to pay for that? And once she's home, I just intuitively feel strongly that once she gets there you're going to know that she belongs there," Amanda explained.

"It's not going to be like in the past when you've gotten puppies. It's just going to be different. When you get a puppy that's reincarnated, it's so much easier. It's not like you're teaching the puppy new things. You're just reminding them of what they already know. Training is so easy. So, I don't feel like you're going to need to book an appointment either before or after. Trust the process. Have faith that everything is falling together perfectly. Follow Pinto's lead and just be grateful to be on this profound journey with this amazing soul. Just maintain that positive energy. When a puppy comes back, they come back with this energy of, I know what I'm here to do, so let's do it. And especially with Ringo being such a strong, wise soul, there is no part of me that feels like you're in for some kind of mental gymnastics with Ringo as a puppy.

"I'm so excited for what's ahead for the two of you, and for your whole family. This is going to be a really beautiful journey that's ahead for all of you. It's hard to put into words, until you've been through it, how whole your family will feel—even if it doesn't feel like it's not whole now—there's a different feeling of wholeness when a reincarnated dog comes home. It's different than anything I've ever experienced in my life. It's so different when you have an animal who has reincarnated. It feels like a piece of you, that you didn't know was missing, has returned. Expect it to be much smoother than I think you're anticipating it being.

"It's always such a pleasure talking to you both. You two are just such lovely people and you're so good together. You're like the sun and the moon. You're such a complete whole and I love it so much."

With that, we ended the call feeling lighter and more ready.

CHAPTER FORTY

Releasing Ringo.

The weather had warmed a little. The days were longer. The sun was brighter. The time was drawing near that we would be bringing Nina home. We had one last important task to complete before we welcomed this new little body into our lives. We needed to release Ringo's ashes.

There was a special boulder way out in the middle of Sycamore Canyon. Ringo loved to hike out there with George, sit on the giant rock, and enjoy the peaceful vibe of looking out over this vast canyon. The two of them would sit there together, enjoying the wave of satisfaction washing over both of them. Best friends enjoying one another, enjoying life. Sometimes, the whole family would make this hike to sit atop this special perch. Ringo welcomed Matty and Pinto to the party, and of course, he always loved it when mom tagged along.

This was the place we chose to release the remains of his physical body. George carried the beautiful wooden box, decorated with interesting patterns carved into the wood. The box was weighty.

Rather than walking in silence, we told stories of Ringo's life. We laughed, we cried, we stopped to hug each other, we noted places on the trail where Ringo had chased a bunny, held off a coyote, cornered a rat, and ran unabashedly off the trail and into the hills.

When we got to the Ringo Rock, our emotions had been spent and we felt ready to open the box, take out the plastic bag that contained ashes and a few small bone fragments. We tossed his remains into the wind and let it scatter our boy onto the ground that he loved. This would be his perfect resting place.

We now felt ready to welcome the vast soul that was Ringo back into our family in the body of tiny little Nina.

CHAPTER FORTY-ONE

Homecoming Day.

As you know, dear reader, my husband George is a dog trainer. From time to time, he will bring another dog home to meet our dogs. It's a small part of what he offers to a client whose dog is in the process of being socialized. Many times, the dog is a puppy.

When a puppy comes to visit, that pup usually enters our yard with caution. He walks slowly. He assesses things cautiously. It takes a while for him to feel comfortable. This is how our dogs react: Pinto runs over to the new dog, gives a little bark, runs around to engage, offers a little pee-mail, then backs off to kind of ignore our visitor. Matty runs to the dog, sniffs him up and down, plays a little chase if he can engage our visitor, then goes on about his business with no further engagement. This is perfect behavior for a dog who is timid or under-socialized. Matty and Pinto are non-threatening. They are friendly, but not overly so. A dog who is new to the experience is helped to feel calm.

The day we brought Nina home, we witnessed something entirely different.

George went into the backyard with little Nina in his arms. He sat down on the ground with her, allowing her a little time to explore. She didn't wander far from his lap, and returned frequently to her new safe place. When we thought the timing was right, we let Matty and Pinto into the yard. What we witnessed then was nothing short of miraculous.

Nina ran to Matty and Pinto, and they to her. To say all three tails were wagging ferociously is an understatement. Their entire bodies were wriggling and wagging from head to toe. They were licking one another, letting out little whimpers of joy. They began to run and chase one another. There was so much love, so much joy. This was definitely a reunion. We were witnessing the reunion of best friends, of siblings who had been separated and were now reunited. There was no question about it. Our Ringo had come back to us. Our hearts were healed.

CHAPTER FORTY-TWO

It's Puppy Time!!!

To say that Nina was an adorable puppy is clearly an understatement. She was everything we could have dreamed of. She had all the puppy goofiness. She loved to play, chew, make messes, give us adorable high-pitched barks, and romp with her brothers. But she also demonstrated characteristics that were very Ringo-esque.

We put a tall, metal baby fence around the perimeter of our family room. The purpose was to contain a little pup who would have no consistent bladder control until about six months. This gave her plenty of room to play, nap, eat, and enjoy the company of her family. We moved all the furniture out of the contained area and set up camping chairs and metal TV trays. This allowed one of us, and many times both of us, to sit with her, play with her and begin to train her. We called the family room "Nina's World."

We had set up a crate and a dog bed within the confines of Nina's World. She had several squeaky toys to chew on and play catch with. One day, George began to toss the toys into her crate, one at a time. He tossed a toy in and then said, "Nina, get your toy and take it to your bed." This eleven-week-old puppy did exactly that. Each toy was joyfully retrieved from the crate and taken to be stacked on the bed. She performed this task, on command, seamlessly, with seven stuffed toys. There was no previous training to teach her to do this, she just knew. She was clearly tapping into her Ringo memory bank.

Nighttime is always challenging with a new puppy. The whole family has been attentive to their every need during the day. At night, when it's time for everyone to go to bed, this is when a puppy will cry, or bark, or howl when left alone. George was well-trained in how to best orient a puppy to sleeping at night. He made a commitment to sleep downstairs in the guest bedroom. He bought a small, puppy-sized crate and set it up on the left side of the guest room bed. He slept on the right side. Nina whimpered just a little when put into her crate, but George was right there, sleeping next to her throughout the night. If she stirred and indicated that she needed to relieve herself during the night, he could easily take her out into the yard to do her business.

This sleeping arrangement continued for about three months after which time Nina would graduate to a large crate positioned next to the other dogs' crates. She seemed comfortable to sleep in the crate that was once hers when she was in her Ringo body. She was a big girl now and could sleep for about a five-hour stretch before barking to go out to go potty. Little by little, she became potty trained and only made messes in the house a couple of times a week. (It's a process.)

George and I took Nina to as many places as we could to continue her socialization. She was not a shy puppy. She was joyful and outgoing. She loved meeting new people and became a great ambassador for the breed.

Almost every day, George and I would discover another little quirky behavior in Nina that was clearly a Ringo trait. She had his eyes, his intensity, his love for TV, his voice.

Ringo's bark was loud and kind of scary. When he wanted something, like a treat or to engage in play, he would bark loudly. I didn't like this, so I taught him how to use his "inside voice." If he barked loudly, I only had to say, "quietly" or "use your inside voice" and he would whisper bark. I tried this with Nina when she was still young and, of course, she complied right away.

CHAPTER FORTY-THREE
What About Two Border Collies?

During our first few weeks with Nina, we relied on our breeders, Orshi and Frank, to guide us into the intricacies of raising a border collie puppy. Yes, we had done this before with Ringo, but all these years later, it somehow seemed brand new. They were a great help to us and we became friends.

Many times, on a Saturday or Sunday morning, Orshi and Frank would come over for a playdate. They would bring one or two of their adult dogs, and a couple of puppies. One puppy they brought every time was Abbie, Nina's little sister. The bond these two littermates had was undeniable. They loved running around our backyard at breakneck speeds, having been infected by "the zoomies." They played to the point of exhaustion, then came to check in with a human then back to playing, then checking in again.

It was always a joy when they were here, and a little sad when they left. We especially missed Abbie.

One day, George had an idea. "Hey, why don't we ask Orshi if Abbie can have a sleepover. Maybe she could spend the weekend with us."

We called, asked our question, and Orshi said, "Would you like to keep her longer than a weekend? Maybe seven or eight days? Frank has to go out of town and one less pup will make less work for me." And so, our sweet little furry house guest came to stay.

What a week that was. The pups had a great time playing chase, wrestling, and doing training games with George. We took them both on little hiking adventures, and did fun things to advance their socializing.

Abbie was quite shy when we were out and about. She was even a tiny bit shy with us. The pups were now seven-months-old. Nina had been socializing since she was 12-weeks-old. Abbie had not had the benefit of getting out. Young pups need to be exposed to people, other dogs, loud noises, unexpected sights, traffic—lots of things to help them learn that the world can be a safe place. She hadn't been exposed to all the things Nina had. Abbie, in fact, had been chosen by Orshi and Frank to be one of their breeding females. Her life would be limited. She would compete in the show ring to gain titles, and when she was a little over two years old she would be bred and begin whelping litters.

Abbie was such a sweet little dog. Though still quite shy, her temperament was friendly and always cheerful. Her personality was so different from Nina. Abbie was light-hearted and cheerful. Nina was intense. Abbie moved like a lithe little gazelle. She could run like the wind, turn on a dime, always carrying her body in a manner that suggested she was happy and carefree. There was such a difference in the behavior of the two pups, we gave them nicknames befitting their personalities. Abbie's nickname was "Sparkles" and we called Nina "Clint" after Clint Eastwood. We chose this for Nina because whenever she was waiting for a game of chase, or waiting for a ball to be thrown, she employed the most intense look, complete with squinted eyes and an air of danger.

George began to take Abbie out for gentle, guarded walks around an outdoor neighborhood mall where she could see people and dogs at a distance. He also drove her to a neighborhood park where they would sit together in the front seat of George's Scion. We called this "doggie TV" because Abbie could sit on George's very safe lap and lean into him as she observed the big world of people, dogs, soccer, and jungle gym from behind the windshield of her car.

With all this focused attention, Abbie began to blossom. We could witness her coming out of her shell more each day. Seeing her gain confidence and begin to move through her little life with more self-assurance made us wish that she could stay with us forever. We hated the thought of her going back to the more confined environment of her home with Orshi and Frank. They would take good care of this little girl, helping her to whelp beautiful puppies, but we wanted her to grow into the full expression of her personality out in the big, beautiful world. We started to fantasize about keeping Abbie.

On about the tenth day of Abbie's "sleepover", we called Orshi to find out what the plans were for getting her back home. Would they pick her up or would we deliver her? When George talked to Orshi, she said, "How would you like to keep her longer?" "How long?" we asked. "Hmmm... forever?" Orshi asked. George and I looked at each other, wide-eyed. "Do you mean forever like a couple of months, or do you mean this could be her forever home?" "Her forever home," she said.

Oh my God, oh my God, oh my God!!! We were so excited we could hardly speak. We said, "Yes! Yes!! Yes!!!" This would be Abbie's home.

It wasn't quite as clean cut as it appeared. We met with Orshi and Frank. They still wanted her to be bred and whelp two litters of puppies. The arrangement would be that she would be our dog, but when she came into her second or third heat after her second birthday, she would be bred. The details were spelled out like this: She would go to Orshi and Frank's for breeding. She would live with us throughout her pregnancy, then she would go back to Orshi and Frank to whelp the puppies. She would live with them to raise her pups until they were ready to go to their own forever homes, at about nine weeks, then she could come home to us.

We wanted her so badly, not so much because we couldn't live without her. We wanted her because we wanted to give her the full, rich life that she deserved.

We signed the papers and Abbie became ours.

Both Nina and Abbie were seven months old and we soon realized they were a huge handful. Backyard zoomies were a regular occurrence. They wrestled and chased one another in the house. They jumped up and over furniture. They barked every time someone walked their dog past our house, and always at the kind Amazon people. There were potty accidents in the house. To say it was chaos was an understatement. There were times that we wondered if we had made a mistake in adding Abbie to our family. *Would it always be this chaotic?*

George hunkered down and created a training plan and we both went to work. We had to take them off separately for training and exercise sessions because they were so bonded with one another that, if together, they would ignore us. Little by little, it all became manageable. They learned indoor and outdoor manners. They learned that relaxation could be pleasurable, that they didn't always have to be on the go. An optimum daily schedule began to reveal itself. We signed Abbie up for scent training and Nina for agility classes. Months had passed and finally, it became a real pleasure to move through life with these two magnificent pups.

We circled back to being happy that Abbie was with us, but the fact that we had signed a contract for her to have two litters of puppies began to loom over our heads. We were now deeply in love with Abbie and so happy that she had become well-adjusted, it was impossible to think of her being gone from us for any amount of time, let alone over two months at a stretch when she gave birth. We began to hope that Orshi and Frank would change their minds. In fact, we dropped a couple of hints and when they were brushed aside, we wrote an email asking if they would change their minds. The answer was clearly, no.

Life went on and the pups grew into one-year-olds. A little before their first birthday, they each went into heat and chaos ensued. The flood of hormones in their system made them, well... bitchy. They each became more protective of their territories, their toys, their beds, and their humans. There were little fights over food and toys, and one day at the park, they got into a huge fight over a ball. We were counting the days until they could be spayed, but that wouldn't happen for almost another year for Nina, and a few years beyond that for Abbie. We went through two heat cycles with each pup, and then Nina turned eighteen months old.

Eighteen months was the magic age. Until then, puppy's bones are growing, their joints are becoming fully developed. If they are spayed before this growth is complete, there could be ugly things like dysplasia, weak tendons, and arthritis in their future. We counted the days and finally at eighteen months and twelve days (but who was counting??) Nina was spayed. This made a difference in her personality. It just kind of took the edge off.

CHAPTER FORTY-FOUR
No Puppies for Sparkles.

The months ticked by. We added Abbie to the training roster at the agility camp. Both pups were coming along nicely in negotiating the obstacles and paying attention to me. I was the one who trained with the girls. I was the one who ran them at class and during our practice sessions. For whatever reason, George decided he wanted to be my back-up, but didn't want to run the dogs himself. It was just as well because I loved it. We drove to our training camp four times each week; twice for classes and twice to practice.

During the period of time between the girl's first and second birthday, we kept in touch with Orshi and Frank. Though they were still committed to breeding Abbie, one of their prize females whelped a pup that would be perfect for the show ring. Her name was Ruby and she was, indeed, a gem. We were hoping she would usurp Abbie as the prized breeding bitch.

Sure enough, I got a brief text from Orshi saying they had found the perfect girl for their breeding line. Abbie was off the hook. She didn't have to produce any litter. She didn't have to leave her home.

We quickly made an appointment to have her spayed before any minds could be changed. Abbie was ours, one hundred percent our pup. No contractual agreement beyond the doors of our home and the huge space she filled in our hearts.

CHAPTER FORTY-FIVE

Don't Miss Me. I'm Right Here. I'm Ringo.

The months churned on, and our adventures with the two girls became even more magical. We decided to speak to Ringo now that he was in his new Nina body. We were also curious as to whether his reincarnation had something to do with our certainty that Abbie was also destined to be our girl. We called Amanda.

We asked if Ringo's soul is partially in Nina and partially in Abbie. Maybe we were compelled to get them both because it was part of Ringo's guidance. Amanda said she has come to know that it's possible that a dog's soul can split into two animals.

Amanda put us on hold for two to three minutes while she talked to Nina.

"It's crazy how much she reminds me of Ringo. I know it's the same soul but it's almost challenging for me to recognize that he's in a different body, even as I'm looking at the photo. It's just so bizarre how much his energy is so fluid. The way I see the two, there's just no break," she began.

"The reason I'm saying this is because it's very often that I communicate with an animal in a different body and there are some big changes between them, meaning that the animal's soul has made adjustments from the time they left one body and got into another one. And it doesn't feel that way at all to me. It feels completely fluid. There is not a bump in the road."

She asked Nina, "Sweetheart, how are you enjoying life in this new body? Your parents have a lot of questions, and I want to give you the floor first."

"Well, I absolutely love this life. I loved my last life, and this one is even more exciting."

"What makes it more exciting?"

"It is so fulfilling. I feel as though my parents both, collectively—they both understand me on such a more complete level. I feel I'm inside out sometimes," Nina said.

"What do you mean by inside out?"

(I'm sorry, I'm going to refer to Nina as a he because I'm experiencing her as Ringo, and I'm having a hard time saying she," Amanda explained.)

"I feel like I'm inside out sometimes," Nina said. "I feel like they're looking at my soul so much that they're looking at my soul more than they're looking at my body. It's a really great feeling."

"Tell me a little bit about how you feel about the existence of being in this puppy body. Tell me what life is like, the ins and outs of daily life."

"Well, it's perfect. What do you want me to say? Are you waiting for a complaint? I don't know what to say then, I'll just be real quiet because I don't have anything to complain about."

Amanda asked him if he intended on his sister being there on purpose or was it happenstance from his perspective. Did he want to share with her if they are one soul, have they been together before or did he need to save her? Would her fate have been something different—an unfortunate fate or a terrible home eventually—had she stayed where she was?

"I'm just curious. I feel there is always more to it than our human version of it," Amanda told us.

She puts us on hold to ask Nina a few more questions.

"Sweetheart, tell me a little bit about your relationship with this other dog. Are you two one soul? Your parents and I are very curious. We're presuming your soul is in two bodies. Is that the case?"

He said, "Do you mean my soul, as it was Ringo is also in her as well?"

"Yes, besides being in Nina's body, are you also in this other dog's body as well? Is your soul, as Ringo, split into two bodies?"

"My soul Ringo, the soul that you're talking to now, is fully and completely, absolutely, every drop of it squeezed into the body I'm in now. There is not even the tiniest drop in her body," was his answer.

"Okay, so explain to me a bit about that, I'm curious," Amanda asked Nina.

"Can we talk about that in another minute? I want to talk about something important right now, and it's the most important thing. I want my parents to completely acknowledge me as Ringo. I don't want them to think about me as before, because I'm not before, I'm NOW. I'm here. There are times when my parents still miss me as Ringo but that's silly because I'm here. It's like I got a facelift. So, you can't miss something that still is. Do you understand that's an oxymoron? I don't want them to feel as though, at times, they're walking down memory lane mentally and feeling a bit sad or nostalgic."

"It feels like a longing," Amanda told us. "That's what he's showing me, that you're feeling that way sometimes—not all the time, but sometimes—and when he feels that energy being expressed, it really disappoints him greatly because he says how can you be missing him when he is right here?"

"They can't say they miss me at all. They can't think about what was and have a longing. They can't do that. What they can do is, they can miss that moment in time, but they can't miss me. Do you understand the difference?" He continued, "They are worlds apart, and for me they are a feeling of understandable nostalgia versus a feeling of, don't you get me?

I'm standing right in front of you. Thankfully, those moments only come in flashes and they're not often, maybe about once a week."

Ringo went on to say, "The tougher part is that I feel as though they understand me completely, all of the time, except in those moments and then they check out of their connection to me standing right in front of them. Isn't that bizarre?"

"Yes, I can see how important this is to you and how much it's causing you a very significant state of frustration and grief, so let me share that with your parents," Amanda told him.

Amanda then said to us, "I want you to really hear this. For him, it's a very big deal when you do that. For him, in the moment that you do that, it's a state of grief and frustration that is astronomical. It may only last one minute, but that one minute is really painful especially because he is so used to feeling the complete opposite. He feels fully understood, but in that moment, he has utter confusion—how are they missing me when I'm right here. Don't they know it's me? Just for that one minute, this is a really intense emotion for him. He wants everyone to understand that even though he is in this new Nina body, he is still Ringo, this eternal Soul is still Ringo."

Amanda then moved on, "I can't get over how much Ringo is Ringo in this new body. Let me ask him if he'll share a little about his relationship with his sister. Give me just a moment."

When she came back, she relayed that it was difficult to get him to move off our last subject. He said, once again, that he needs for us to recognize him as him in every moment.

"For them to not recognize that it's me, wholeheartedly, that negates the depth of our love." He continued, "Of course, I came back. Of course, I decided I would be with them forever. Of course, we're one unit as a Soul Family. Of course, we're destined to always take care of one another. For them to question, even in a moment, that I'm me, is invalidating our whole purpose together and it brings me such a deep tear in my heart. Do you feel like there's a tear in my heart?"

Amanda said, "Yes, sweetheart, I do. I feel like someone just tore a little piece of your heart out."

"Yes, it physically hurts. It makes me feel like, in that moment, I'm having like a heart palpitation. Any moment that they question who I am is questioning everything that we have together and it breaks my heart."

We (Kathy and George) said that we understood, that we honored his feelings, and that we would never do it again.

To that, he replied, "I hear them that they'll never do it again, and I accept that they didn't do it on purpose, and we don't ever have to talk about this again, and tell them thank you so much for honoring and respecting how valuable this is for me. This is the most important thing that I've said because it weighs really heavy on me and it caused me a deep pain." He added, "It is also important that they acknowledge this to other people. This is an important lesson for the greater good. Humans need to know that the Soul lives on. It is eternal."

He then said, "Okay, I want to talk now about some funner stuff. I want to talk about how much I absolutely love learning and how much I love learning from my dad. I love us being attentive to one another. I try for him to hear me at all times and I try really hard for him to communicate with me, and for him to understand that I'm trying to communicate back."

Amanda told us, "He shows me that he does this thing where he gives you a muzzle punch, but he's trying to get you to really connect with him like, hey, I'm here, do you see me? Pay attention to me. And he wants you to know that he wants to soak up everything that you are giving him. It's really important to him that George understands how much he loves that bonding time."

"There are times that I would even like tough love in difficult moments, and to be rewarded with a 'good boy' for doing it right. Those 'good jobs' are a huge reward because I appreciate the discipline in those moments," Ringo told Amanda.

"He shows me that he needs structure. He needs for you to say, 'Come on; you could do a little better. You're not doing your best. You're doing okay, but that wasn't your best. You can try better.' He thrives on that and he says, push him a little more."

Amanda then asked him, "Do you want to talk to me about your relationship with your sister?"

And he said, "Oh gosh, we're getting to that, can we just go in my order and not yours?"

"Yes, we can definitely go in your order. What's the next thing on the menu?"

"We were going to talk about my sister, but I wanted to be the one to say what we were talking about now."

"So, you tell me. You talk and I'll listen," Amanda acquiesced.

Here's what he said, "Okay, well, I want to show you the difference in our relationship. Do you know how my parents complement one another?"

"Yes, they seem like they're very different."

"Let me show you a snapshot of our relationship."

"He shows me a snapshot of a human relationship. He shows me a police officer and a nurse. They are very different but they go together like yin and yang—they complement one another very well. When he shows me his relationship with his sister there is a yin and a yang. Their personalities are very different and they really complement one another," Amanda shared what she was visualizing.

"I chose for her to be here and she chose to be here because, like my parents' relationship, we are very different. We are compatible in perfect ways but our personalities are very different. One complements the other one. You know, it's like we're making one another whole when we are together. I want you to see it as, I am this soul in this body. I'm Nina. And my sister is a very different soul. She has been with us in previous lifetimes. But she always came to complement me. She is the softer, more feminine version of me. We are very different, personality-wise, and that is a testament to the fact that we're very different souls. Do we match each other? Yes. Have we been together in previous lifetimes? Yes. Does she have characteristics that I find to be similar to Ringo? Not really. She doesn't remind me of who I was in my last lifetime. She reminds me of someone who is meant to complement this lifetime as Nina."

"He shows me that their personalities are very different but they bring out the best in one another. He doesn't see her as like Ringo in any way, so, for him, he wonders how you can think, 'She might be me when she's nothing like me. I'm like Ringo. She's not like me. Is she a soulmate of ours? Yes. Was she meant to be here? Yes.' But to him, there is no part of her or her personality that is reminiscent of who Ringo was last lifetime."

Amanda asked us, "Does Abbie's personality remind you of Ringo?"

We both say an emphatic, "No, not at all."

I started to explain to Amanda why we were confused about, "who is Ringo?" But she stopped me and said, "Let me ask Nina/Ringo if he wants to share with me why he thinks you are questioning this before you tell me. I'm curious if he knows why. I don't want to cut you off, Kathy, but let's hear from Ringo first, then I want to hear what you guys have to say. Let's see if we can get some validation here."

Amanda returned with this information. "When I asked him if he wanted to share with me a little bit about why you felt as though his sister was him, he said, 'Well, it's so silly and it's so insignificant. It's a matter of numbers.' And I asked, 'What do you mean?'"

"It's a matter of numbers. I don't really know how to explain it because it's one of those weird things that humans do, that they count numbers. You know, we don't do that here."

"In the dog world or in the spirit world?

"Neither."

"So, for him it has something to do with numbers. Maybe it could be the time of their birth, the date of their birth?? Something around numbers."

Both George and I laughed, and I said, "Are you ready?"

"Yes, I'm ready and I'm confused," Amanda replied.

"We can clear up the confusion."

We told Amanda the story of how Ringo told us he was coming back as a 33 pound female. What started to confuse us is that Nina was weighing in at 35 pounds and Abbie at 33, so we started to question whether Abbie could be Ringo's soul. Even though Nina acted completely like Ringo, and Abbie did not. Then, as they grew and became more active, Nina settled in at 33 pounds and Abbie as 31 pounds. It was exactly a numbers situation."

Amanda said, "Wow! Wow! Wow!!! It's a matter of numbers. I love that!!!"

Ringo/Nina then said, "I really want to share with you how much I love this lifetime, how much I'm enjoying being in this body, and how much I love having this companion. As much as I love my parents and my siblings, the most important thing for me is that my soul is where I belong. My soul is here with them. It's not just about being with them. It's about us being together and my parents understanding that I came back to share another lifetime with them."

He continued, "I also want to share with you how much I really, really, really love—I really love my sister. She is so pretty."

"And I said yes, as I was laughing," Amanda told us. "And he said, 'Then why are you laughing when I say that?' And I answered, 'I'm laughing because you two are almost identical. You are so similar looking—it's going to make me cry—it's so cute the way you're describing her.'"

(Amanda started to cry and said, "I'm sorry, I get so emotional when I get so much emotion coming from the animals.")

"It's really cute that you're describing her as so pretty because you two look so identical," Amanda repeated to Ringo.

"Oh, no, no, no, just let me be really clear with this for you, I'm ridiculously handsome. I'm five stars. I'm as good looking as they come, but she's really beautiful in a different kind of way. I feel like she has this femininity about her. When I look at her, I see these eyelashes."

"And he shows me that he sees her like her eyes are almost like having eyeliner on. That's how he pictures her when he's looking at her," Amanda said. "I don't visually see that in her picture, but he sees it when he looks at her. He sees this more feminine eyelash. Then he said, 'I see myself as a boy; do you see it that way?' And I said, 'Yes, absolutely.'"

Ringo went on, "Can I tell you something else about her? I find it endearing. She's a little bit of an airhead. She's a little bit of a bubblehead. She looks like, 'Oh my God, really guys??' She has this look and her eyes get really wide and it's real cute. It's like she's saying, 'Hey guys, really guys, hey guys.' Isn't that cute? She's cute."

"Is she playing dumb because she thinks it's cute for you to play dumb?" Amanda asked him.

"No, she's not playing dumb. She's not playing. She's just a little bit more simple than I am. She doesn't have the depth that I have."

"Well, that's very sweet. Are you in love with her?"

"Of course, I am. What kind of question is that? She is my mate."

"I got it. You're not just seeing her as like your sister and your litter mate. You're seeing her as like your wife, your girlfriend."

"I totally have a crush on her," Ringo said.

"That's very interesting. You know, in the human world that would be..." Amanda began.

"Oh, I don't want to talk about the human world and things being taboo because the thing about it is, I love her, and I've been in love with her before and we were destined to be together again in this lifetime and I'm so excited we get to share our lives together again. I'm really happy that I got some time alone with my parents before she came so that they could really get to know me, so that they could really see that I am Ringo, and so that my personality can really develop, and that bond can really develop. I am so happy that there was a gap in time before she came in. And I love her. I'm in love with her. And I want them to know that I see her as they see one another. They're each other's mate. Each other's partner. And that's how I see her. I love her very much and I love her dopey doe-eyed face that she makes. It's just adorable."

"Okay, let me share this with your parents."

Amanda turned back to us, "So, do you understand that he sees himself so fully as a male that I had a hard time saying she and that he also sees himself as her boyfriend, like he's the man in the relationship. And they're in love and they're best friends. It's almost like watching them reminds me (oh, I'm getting so emotional—this is so sweet—such a sweet communication for me today). He sees her as—he's so in love with her that I feel like

I'm watching two 12-year-olds be in love. Like two 12-year-old neighbors fell in love with each other. They're out riding bikes but the story is that they grow up, fall in love and get married, and live happily ever after. I feel like I'm watching two human soulmates running around catching fireflies and riding their bikes as children, knowing that their love is not just a schoolyard crush, but it really is a soulmate connection. That's how I feel when I watch Ringo with his Abbie."

Ringo wanted to speak a little more about this. "There really should be no attention paid to gender or pronouns. Humans need to understand how paper-thin gender is. It's loose. It's fluid. One important lesson I've come to teach humans is that they should make gender roles non-existent. Soul is flexible. There is a thin veil between gender identity. Everything is very loose."

*He continued, "Other people's work on this—documentaries and such— they're getting it all wrong. Their thinking is misplaced. There is a better idea that needs to germinate. The term that I like is not transgender. It's **transunion**, the act of souls coming together, uniting, no matter what their gender. Tell my mom it's her job to write, teach, lead, sing about this. The very act of my rebirthing from a male body to a female body, yet still expressing my true Soul. This will be a teaching tool in itself."*

When I asked how I should do this, he said, "Just channel Ringo/Nina when you write. I'll be present to guide you."

CHAPTER FORTY-SIX

Abbie's Turn to Talk with Amanda.

We asked to turn the conversation to Abbie. We wanted her to ask, "How is she feeling? What do we need to know about her?"

Amanda tuned into Abbie and told us that her energy is that of a lighter, younger soul. Her energy is light, happy, not nearly as complex as Nina. "Ringo brings a lot of old wisdom. He's very intelligent. Abbie is just plain lovely. She's simple, sweet, authentic, and a little naïve." Amanda tells us that her energy is just so pure. "She has a lot of happy energy."

She asked Abbie to tell us a little about herself. This is what she told us was Abbie's reply:

"I am in the best-case scenario life. I hit the jackpot of lives. I'm living with my Soul Family and I get to spend every day with my baby, my sweetheart." Here she was referring to Ringo/Nina.

"She shows me that in previous lifetimes they were together and she was always the softer, more feminine dog. She has always been the perfect complement to Nina, and it's no different in this lifetime. She is the yin to Nina's yang. They're soulmates. They're twin flames. She is so grateful that it all turned out perfectly for the two of them to be born together as littermates so that they can spend their entire physical lives together.

"She shows me that she is easily stimulated by outside sounds and anything that excites her. Her energy is 'on' much of the time. She likes to run with the birds when they're flying over. She likes to guard the house and bark when anyone is coming near that might be a threat. She tells me that she likes her crate. She often feels mentally overwhelmed. She sees her crate as a safe space where she doesn't have to pay attention. She shows me that her crate helps her to mentally decompress."

"What I would like," Abbie told Amanda, "is more alone time. I love to be with my family and I love to be in the thick of things, but I would also like more alone time. I like the darkness in my crate. It helps me decompress."

Amanda asked Abbie what else she would like to tell us about herself. "Sometimes it bothers me that I have to pay really close attention to learn things. I feel like I'm a slow learner compared to Nina and Matty."

"Since Abbie brought up Matty, I told her that her parents said she seems to head-butt with Matty at times. I asked her to tell me about that," Amanda said.

"I don't head-butt with Matty. I just jump at him a little," Abbie said. "Matty puts off this energy like he thinks he's special and sometimes that annoys me so I jump at him. Maybe I feel a little jealous."

Amanda then asked how she felt about Pinto, and Abbie said, "I'm intrigued by Pinto. I feel like he gets me better than anyone else. He doesn't get over-stimulated and he tells me that he had to try really hard to learn. He told me that once upon a time he was a dingbat, but that he's settled into it now and he learns things better. He's kind of like a mentor to me."

Amanda told us, "It would be good if you would work with each of them separately. Spend time with Abbie alone so that she gets what she needs but doesn't feel the weight of expectation or comparing her to one of the other dogs. She needs time away from the other dogs. She told me that she likes being talked to when she doesn't have to respond. Just talk to her as you're doing something. She will love that and it will calm her. She also wants time alone, away from the other dogs."

Before we ended our talk with Abbie, she told Amanda, "Nina needs extra quality time with mom and dad, you know. She requires more, I require less. Nina needs simple, goofy playtime as well as training. I need some alone time with mom and dad. And I love my crate."

All of this was true about our little Abbie June. She was delightfully happy. The word alacrity comes to mind. Brisk and cheerful readiness. That was Abbie. Always ready and always cheerful. And yes, she loves her crate and she loves to chase the birds.

CHAPTER FORTY-SEVEN

Matty Leaves His Body.

And so, our Soul Family is together again. Through Amanda, we have come to have a depth of understanding of who each of our dogs and cats are, how their soul energy expresses in their physical being, and how we share an unbreakable bond that has moved through lifetimes together. What a gift. What an incredible gift. Not only has our bond deepened with each of our animals, but for me, it has created an exponential love affair with all beings.

I find myself talking to the coyotes I pass on the bike trail and the hawks that fly overhead or stop to watch me pass. I take time to connect with the wild burros that populate our neighborhood. I even talk to the spiders I find in the garden or scurrying across the garage floor. When I walk through our neighborhood, I speak to the dogs whose noses pop through their backyard gates. I take a moment to commune with the cats who sit on neighborhood lawns. And, of course, my diet is plant-based. How could I ever eat an animal who I now know, without a doubt, has a soul and is a sentient being? All the cows, all the pigs, the chickens, the turkeys, the fish. All, each and every one, deserves the fullest, most freedom-filled life we can possibly give them.

Amidst all the glorious play, the time spent running in the park, playing chase and fetch, the hours we logged in agility classes, hanging out on the couch together in the evening, employing "doggy TV", there was one horribly sour note. Matty's happy little light was fading.

Matthew Patrick was now almost thirteen. He had become intermittently disoriented. His hearing and vision had dulled. His musculoskeletal system was giving out. He had a hard time lifting up to standing and walking. He was becoming incontinent. We knew it was time. We called *Lap of Love*.

As the kind veterinarian sat down on our family room floor, she talked to Matty in a low, calming voice. She stroked his head as he weakly wagged his tail. His fur had become so scruffy with old age and his tail was showing signs of hair loss.

The vet listened to us as we described Matty's daily routines and the discomfort he seemed to carry. She agreed that we were making the right decision in helping him make his journey across the Rainbow Bridge.

She administered the injection that sedated him, and then the injection that eased his life-force right out of his body. No matter how many times we had been through this, there was nothing that made it any easier and, as he took his last breath, we all wept. Nina, Abbie, and Pinto sat close and were invited to come and say their last goodbyes to their sweet brother.

CHAPTER FORTY-EIGHT
Matty in the Afterlife.

Three weeks had passed and we were missing Matty terribly. We decided to call Amanda and check in with Matty.

Amanda told us, "This is an interesting conversation because Pinto wants to talk first. He tells me that Matty's body was gone, but his spirit remained for about three days after he passed. In fact, he asked Pinto, 'How did I leave? Did somebody help me?' Pinto said he was relieved for Matty because he knew that there was a lot of pain and confusion toward the end of Matty's life. After witnessing both Ringo and Matty being assisted in releasing their physical body, Pinto told me, 'I want my mom and dad to promise that they'll help me when the time comes. I don't want my body to malfunction like Matty and Ringo.'

"Pinto is deeply saddened by the loss of Matty, but Nina is his powerhouse. Nina helps Pinto to feel safe. And Pinto's opinion of Matty has changed so much over the years. He now describes Matty as clever, kind, funny, sweet. Pinto says Matty was easy to love. He was never in a bad mood," Amanda said.

"I love him very much and I miss hanging out and taking naps with him, but I'm relieved for him because I know how exhausted his body was," Pinto told her.

Pinto went on to tell Amanda that he needs to be babied.

"Pinto needs time to just hang out with Nina because she knows how to make everyone feel better. And he says he also needs some alone time to mourn. He says that he has been cuddling with Solo. She hangs out with Pinto, and her spirit creates a kind of sacred space in your house. It's her way of still being comforting in the home. He really hopes that Matty will join them soon," Amanda told us.

"Pinto also says that he loves his time with 'the two Magoons'. He loves to be with them because they are conscious of his needs and their energy feels happy, light, and optimistic," Amanda said.

We all wondered where this phrase "the two Magoons" came from. How did Pinto come up with that name for the border collies? I looked it up and learned that Magoon is a surname of Scottish origin. This was actually perfect because border collies originate from the land bordering Scotland and England. How did Pinto know this?

It was time to connect to Matty. Amanda tuned in to his energy and here is what he had to say:

"I need my family to know that I am in a state of blissful nothingness. I'm completely enchanted and I'm really enjoying this high vibrational state. I feel very whole. I am in a pure bliss state. I would like my family to meet me here. For my mom, it might be done through meditation. For my dad, he can get there when he's in the zone on his bike."

Amanda told us that he would like for us to just feel the beautiful state alongside him. "Don't speak his name or visualize him because that pulls him out of this state and brings him back to a more solid, earthly energy. He just wants you all to experience this bliss state with him.

"He tries to describe the state that he finds himself in. He says he can compare it to the roller coaster adrenaline rush of a mountain bike ride, or a really deep comfy nap, or being in love or taking a bite out of the most delicious, forbidden food. All of this combined is the bliss state he is in. He says that these are ways we can get into this bliss state with him: the adrenaline of extreme sports, a deep, comfy nap, enjoying being in love, and eating scrumptious food."

Matty began to philosophize a little. He began to talk about selflessness versus selfishness. "Selflessness is made up. It doesn't serve you. When you do this, you're changing your DNA. The takers of the world came up with this fallacy." Matty continued, "Fill yourself up!! Be self-serving. Take good care of yourself. Here is the truth: Selflessness is opposite to the state of bliss. It's like living in shame. It ruins everything."

Matty further told us that "the toddlers" (meaning the border collies) will have to take care of Pinto now because he is not able to do it.

"He may be able to bring his spirit back into your home one day, but for now, he doesn't want to be disturbed. If you want to connect with him, you must meet him where he is," Amanda shared Matty's thoughts.

And finally, Matty told Amanda, "Tell my parents that their lives are a blank page. We are all such creators of our life. Tell my parents to make something beautiful to put into the world. Create something beautiful."

CHAPTER FORTY-NINE
Checking in with Tinker.

We turned to Tinker. "How is she doing?" I asked.

Amanda tuned in to Tinker's energy. She told Tinker that her mom and dad are worried that she stays up in the bedroom all the time. "They are concerned that you never come downstairs anymore. They don't want you to feel lonely or isolated. So, sweetheart, how are you feeling about this?"

Tinker told us that she was doing fine. "She feels like she is up high, on her throne," Amanda shared with a little chuckle.

"I am enjoying my life so much," Tinker said. "I get room service twice a day when my mom and dad bring my meals. My bathroom is in the closet, very convenient. I love it up here. Don't try to take me out of this space."

Amanda said that Tinker was enjoying her twilight years. "She is nineteen years old. This is her retirement. Physically, she seems like a much younger cat. Maybe around eleven-years-old. She has a little discomfort when she takes a really deep breath, but on a scale of one to ten, it's only about a two. She also has a little arthritis in her left front wrist.

"Overall, Tinker is happy and content."

"I'm really enjoying this stage of my life. It's like I'm enjoying a relaxed retirement. No one is bothering me, and I don't have to do anything."

"That's great, sweetheart," Amanda replied to Tinker. "Is there anything else you want your parents to know?"

"I like listening to the dogs acting wild. I like listening to any chaos that's around me. I can just listen and I don't have to participate. I really like this. All the sounds around me give me delight."

CHAPTER FIFTY
For the Love of Ringo.

As I look back over the life we've had with these precious beings, my heart feels full; fuller than it has ever felt. Is this Ringo in Nina's body? I can say an emphatic yes to that question.

Beyond all the evidence that has been uncovered through our conversations with Amanda, and all the Ringo mannerisms that are present in Nina, there is a little thing that I do from time to time that confirms it even further for me. Nina will be asleep on a couch or a rug. I'll say a few words that she knows, very quietly, to observe her response. She does nothing but stay in her deep sleep state. Then I'll say "Ringo," quietly, with the same inflection I've used in all the other words I've just said. She immediately opens her eyes, snaps her head around, and looks deeply into my eyes.

Nina sleeps in the bed with me at night. I'm under the covers, she is snuggled in next to me, on top of the covers. Our nightly routine includes a little massage around the ears, the face, down the spine, and, of course, a belly rub and lots of kisses. As I massage her, I talk to her. I tell her that I'm so grateful she chose to come back to us, in her Nina body. I call her Ringo and tell her that I deeply honor all that she is. I tell her that I know she is Ringo, living her best life in the body of Nina. She acknowledges this by kissing my face and putting her paw on my heart. We are in sacred communion with one another.

This love I feel for Nina is multilayered. I love her as my dog. I love her like a child. I love her as my teacher. I love her as my spiritual peer.

Ringo teaches us that gender is fluid. My language around gender has also become fluid. Sometimes I refer to Nina as "her", sometimes "him". I usually call her Nina, but at times I call her Ringo. I think of her as both Nina and Ringo.

I have loved all of my dogs and cats through the years, but the love I feel for Nina feels like so much more. It feels destined. It feels informative. It is sacred. It feels like acknowledging and connecting to something that is so magical, so expansive. I know, without any doubt, that our souls have been connected for many lifetimes. I am grateful for the lessons I am learning from this magnificent dog about life, about love, and about family.

George and I are in our seventies now. I'm seventy-three, George is seventy-five. Nina and Abbie are turning three in about two weeks, at the end of January 2024. We keep ourselves active and healthy. We work with a personal trainer, we mountain bike, we hike, and we do yoga. All of this has greater focus now.

The pups will likely live to be around fifteen. That puts me at eighty-five and George at eighty-seven. We're hoping that all our efforts to remain healthy and robust will carry us into our nineties. We're hoping, like Ringo promised, that we'll all age and begin to slow down together.

George and I have always had a little mantra we say to one another: "Happy Healthy, Happy Healthy, Happy Healthy—Dead Together." We don't want one to make their transition out of body without the other. It would be too painful, so we've created this mantra as an affirmation that we'll go together. Just like the old couple in the movie, *The Notebook*.

In my mind, we now extend this out to Nina and Abbie. I want nothing more than to be fully present for the remainder of the years we have together. And, if I could create the perfect scenario for our transition out of body, it would go something like this:

It's a Sunday afternoon. We all lay down to take a nap together. This is a nap that is deeper than any nap we've ever taken. We begin to breathe in unison. Our strong hearts entrain with one another. They are all beating together. Slowly, steadily, and without fanfare, those beats begin to slow to a complete stop. Our bodies have completed their assignment. We are free of those bodies now. We cross the Rainbow Bridge together.

Nina is leading the way, walking to my right. Abbie is walking to George's left. We feel so light, so joyful, so full of anticipation. And then we see them. Matty, Pinto, Solo, Tinker, Westy, Kiska, and all the other precious beings who have honored us by sharing our lives. They are all there waiting for us.

This is our Soul Family.

This is Love.

About the Author

KATHY BOLTE is an International Yoga Teacher, Mantra Meditation Teacher, Kīrtan Musician, Retreat Leader, and facilitator of Women's Wisdom Circles. She is a featured writer for Elephant Journal, an online publication dedicated to the mindful life.

An avid mountain biker, Kathy hits the bike trails of Southern California at least twice a week. She loves working with her two Border Collies in the extraordinarily fun and challenging sport of dog agility. She lives in Riverside, California with her husband, their three dogs, and their 19-year-old cat.

Acknowledgments

My deepest gratitude goes out to our oh-so-gifted animal communicator, Amanda Reister, without whom I could never have written this book and, more importantly, I could never have truly *known* my beloved dogs and cats.

My heart goes out to the cadre of loving professionals who have cared for our pups and our cats so sweetly. Dr. Jacqueline De Grasse, our doggy chiropractor who saved Matty's life. She is truly an angel. Our agility coaches, Nancy Edwards and Kayana (aka Kay) Therrien, who have guided me through the challenging task of trusting my dogs to know what they're doing on the course. The wonderful folks at Norco Animal Hospital and Riverside Cat Hospital who make sure our fur kids are healthy and happy.

I offer a giant debt of gratitude to Orshi and Frank Horvath, founders and owners of Aleannan Border Collies (formerly known as Overdrive Border Collies). They invited us into their home to meet their pride and joy: the gorgeous dogs in their breeding lineage. These two amazing people have dedicated their lives to careful, selective breeding; holding breed standards at the forefront while also breeding for sweet, gentle temperament. They listened carefully to our story of Ringo coming back into the body of a small female border collie. They embraced the story, embraced us as their friends, and gave Nina and Abbie the best-ever start in life. To be loved, cherished and nurtured from birth is what every dog deserves. We can't thank these two stellar humans enough for giving Ringo his new Nina body, and for gifting Nina with a sweet sister to love forever.

There are several friends who got the call, "Would you please read a few chapters of my book to see if I'm on the right track with my writing?" I am indebted to each of you for holding my hand through this journey. Jacquie Freeman, Laureen Pitman, Georgia Hill, and my sweetheart, George, all jump to the top of this list.

It's sometimes difficult to dedicate time to writing when perched at my desk at home. At any given moment a sweet border collie will land her head in my lap, asking to play. How can I say no? There were many days I had to exit the home scene to get any writing done. I tip my hat to the many coffee shops who hosted my butt in the seat, sipping on a latte or two, writing, writing, and writing. Most especially I thank our little neighborhood coffee brewer: Mundial Coffee. (If you're ever in Riverside, check them out.)

And finally, my family. This story would not be possible without the love and support of my husband, George, who followed his passion to become a dog trainer after retiring from his corporate career. He has taught me so many things about helping our dogs to feel safe, to feel loved, and to honor them for exactly who they are. To our four awesome children, Dania, Zachary, Kelly, Nathan and our six delightful grandchildren, Devon, Riley, Olive, Ryanne, Nathan and Henry. These beautiful beings are the glue that holds my heart so tenderly through each step of my life's journey.